o/p
1976
1st
~~lib~~
$10.00

# VOICES FROM THE SOUTHWEST

*Lawrence Clark Powell, Spring 1976, by Dr. John P. Schaefer*

# VOICES FROM THE SOUTHWEST

*A Gathering
in Honor
of Lawrence Clark Powell*

GATHERED BY
DONALD C. DICKINSON
W. DAVID LAIRD
MARGARET F. MAXWELL

*Northland Press · Flagstaff
Mcmlxxvj*

*This volume was produced
on the occasion of Lawrence Clark Powell's
seventieth birthday*

# CONTENTS

*Illustrations* ix
*Contributors* xi
*Introduction* xiii
*Seventy Suns* xv

HISTORY OF THE SOUTHWEST

*History of the Spanish Southwest* 3
*Authors and Books of Colonial New Mexico* 13
*Voices From the Southwest* 33
*The Faces and Forces of Pimería Alta* 45
*The Fifth World — The Ninth Planet* 55

BOOKS AND PEOPLE OF THE SOUTHWEST

*An Amateur Librarian* 65
*Give This Place a Little Class* 76
*Richard J. Hinton and the American Southwest* 82
*J. Ross Browne and Arizona* 92
*Reflections on the Powell-Harrison Correspondence* 102
*The Making of a Novel* 113
*A Chronology of LCP Keepsakes* 132
*A Checklist of Recently Published Works of LCP* 146

# ILLUSTRATIONS

*Lawrence Clark Powell, 1976* frontispiece

*Spanish Conquistador, sixteenth century* 2

*Captain Don Gaspar De Villagrá* 17

*Saguaro cactus* 64

*White House Ruin: Canyon de Chelly* 131

# CONTRIBUTORS

Ansel Adams is a photographer and author living in Carmel, California

Eleanor B. Adams is Research Professor at large, Emeritus, at the University of New Mexico, Albuquerque.

Sarah Bouquet is employed in a bookstore in Tucson, Arizona. The Gatherers gratefully acknowledge her assistance on the entire project.

José Cisneros is an artist who specializes in Spanish background and lives in El Paso, Texas.

L. D. Clark is Professor of English at the University of Arizona, Tucson.

Richard H. Dillon is Sutro Librarian at the Sutro Library, California State Library, San Francisco.

William Everson is Poet in Residence at the University of California, Santa Cruz, Kresge College, Santa Cruz.

Bernard L. Fontana is Ethnologist at the Arizona State Museum, the University of Arizona, Tucson.

Harwood P. Hinton is Editor of *Arizona and the West,* and Professor of History at the University of Arizona, Tucson.

Paul Horgan is an author and Senior Fellow in Letters, Center for Advanced Studies, Wesleyan University, Middletown, Connecticut.

Al Lowman is Research Associate at the Institute of Texan Cultures at San Antonio, the University of Texas, San Antonio.

Robert Mitchell is International Documents Librarian at the University of Arizona, Tucson.

Ward Ritchie is a printer and publisher living in Laguna Beach, California.

John P. Schaefer is President of the University of Arizona, Tucson.

Marc Simmons is a historian living in Cerrillos, New Mexico.

Frank Waters is an author living in Taos, New Mexico.

Jake Zeitlin is the owner of Zeitlin and Ver Brugge, Booksellers, in Los Angeles.

*The Gatherers:*

Donald C. Dickinson is the Director of the Graduate Library School at the University of Arizona, Tucson.

W. David Laird is University Librarian at the University of Arizona, Tucson.

Margaret F. Maxwell is Associate Professor at the Graduate Library School at the University of Arizona, Tucson.

# INTRODUCTION

❖⧆❖

It is appropriate that a volume of Southwestern studies should be gathered in honor of Lawrence Clark Powell, one of the area's leading essayists and bibliographers. The Southwest has always figured importantly in Powell's writing, including such early works as *Heart of the Southwest, A Southwestern Century, Southwestern Book Trails,* more recently *California Classics* and *Southwestern Classics,* and newest of all, *Arizona, a Guide to the State*. Dr. Powell has staked out the region, one stark and arid, but full of beauty, with scholarly care and sensitivity. Through the years he has offered a variety of trail lures to guide and tempt the reader, who would know more of this dry and wrinkled land.

To know the Southwest, one must know the region's history. Where did the first settlers come from? Who recorded the first accounts of these desert lands? What of the Native Americans? How did early settlers fare and what did they do in order to survive the often cruel conditions under which they lived? Answers to these questions and others are offered by the essays in Part I of this volume by Eleanor Adams, Marc Simmons, Frank Waters, Sarah Bouquet and Bernard Fontana.

What was the place of the writer in the Southwest? Who were the pioneers who chronicled the development of early frontier settlements, and brought books in their baggage? What were libraries like in New Mexico in the early twentieth century? How was it to pursue the booktrade on the Los Angeles frontier in the thirties? These questions are answered in the essays included in Part II of this volume, by Richard Dillon, Harwood Hinton, Ward Ritchie, Paul Horgan, Jake Zeitlin and L. D. Clark.

The essays, a poem by William Everson, photographs by Ansel Adams and John Schaefer, and a drawing by José Cisneros, form a portrait of Powell's favorite country, a country both enduring and to be endured.

The man is tough and sinewy, timeless, like the land, hard to change and ever changing. It is with affection, admiration and appreciation that the editors dedicate this small volume on the Southwest to a man of the Southwest in honor of his seventieth birthday.

D. C. Dickinson
D. Laird
M. Maxwell

# SEVENTY SUNS—TO L.C.P.

## By William Everson

*The lean face*
*lazes in autumnal light;*
*a wintry wisdom flickers in the eyes.*

*But the springtime energies,*
*the blood's delight,*
*flame sunrise in those Arizona skies.*

*And all the books*
*his fingers ever touched*
*glow like the desert quartz in fancy caught.*

*And all the loves*
*his ardent lips once brushed,*
*bloom like the yucca in his winey thought.*

*The body is its beauty,*
*and the mind: —*
*these, his two imperatives included,*

*will shape quintessence*
*of a keener kind,*
*the pall of sadly growing old precluded.*

*Now autumn rainfall*
*quicks the desert green.*

*And seventy suns, enjoined*
*glide on serene.*

# HISTORY OF THE SOUTHWEST

*Spanish Conquistador of the middle 16th century by José Cisneros*

# HISTORY OF THE SPANISH SOUTHWEST:
## PERSONALITIES AND DISCOVERIES

*Eleanor B. Adams*

❧

SPECULATION ABOUT THE FABULOUS FRONTIER of New Spain began early in the Spanish colonial period. In 1536, a few years after Hernán Cortés first saw the wonders of the great city of Tenochtitlán-México, Alvar Núñez Cabeza de Vaca and three other ragged survivors of an ill-fated expedition to Florida found their way back to the capital after incredible wanderings through rugged unknown regions far to the north. Just beyond, so the Indians had told them, were cities even richer than Mexico, the seven golden cities that man had sought for centuries before Europe had even dreamed of the existence of America — cities that had ever receded beyond each new horizon. And so in 1539 Fray Marcos de Niza, guided by the Black, Estebanico, went north through what is now Arizona to western New Mexico. When the eager friar gazed from a distance at one of the Zuñi pueblos, somehow his dazzled eyes transformed the primitive Indian village into a shimmering vision of the seven golden cities of Cibola.

Niza's glowing narrative inspired the 1540 expedition of Francisco Vázquez de Coronado to find another Mexico, a "new" Mexico. In the same year Hernando de Alarcón sailed up the Gulf of California and the Colorado River as far as Yuma. By land Coronado's parties ranged from the Grand Canyon to Kansas. But when the weary disillusioned men returned

*Based on a paper read at the tenth annual meeting of the Western History Association, Santa Fe, 1971.*

to Mexico City after two years of fruitless search and misfortunes, the shame of the colossal failure was so great that the embittered authorities decreed silence about it. Nevertheless, the records and narratives forgotten in dusty files survived, and many of them are now in print.

Forty years were to pass before the Chamuscado-Rodríguez and Espejo expeditions discovered New Mexico for the second time; and fifteen years later, shortly before the turn of the century, don Juan de Oñate added it to the Crown of Spain. Meanwhile explorers and conquerors such as the Ibarras pushed the frontier of New Spain farther and farther north. Profits from the great silver strike at Zacatecas in 1546 were to provide capital for Oñate's conquest of New Mexico in 1598.

The documentary history of the Spanish Southwest is replete with narratives and descriptions by explorers, soldiers, and missionaries. Equally revealing are the many letters, complaints, petitions, special reports, and enormous legal files covering every aspect of frontier life and problems. In them all we find truth, falsehoods, pessimism, well-meaning, if often unjustified, optimism, and sometimes propaganda. Fray Marcos, Pedro de Casteñeda, Diego Pérez de Luxán, Baltasar de Obregón, and Gaspar Castaño de Sosa are some of those who wrote the contemporary narratives and descriptions of the age of discoveries. Gaspar Pérez de Villagrá's *History of New Mexico* tells of the founding of that colony in the most ghastly poesy. Later the Mexican savant don Carlos de Sigüenza y Góngora would scoop the news of the Reconquest in purple prose.

Over the years Franciscan missionary friars covered reams of paper on every conceivable subject. The most famous seventeenth-century firsthand descriptions of New Mexico by a religious are the two memorials of Fray Alonso de Benavides dated 1630 and 1634. Benavides's reports are infinitely useful, but unduly optimistic. He was one of the first promoters of the "Land of Enchantment."

To the southwest the Jesuits had begun the thrust that would carry them over the present Arizona border by the end of the seventeenth century. In 1645 Andrés Pérez de Ribas promoted his Order's cause with a chronicle of the first half-century of missionary *Triumphs* in the Sinaloa area.

It has been said that crucial material for the history of New Mexico was lost in the destruction of the archives in the Pueblo Revolt of 1680. Certainly much of value may be gone forever. But we may thank the bureaucratic tentacles which reached the most remote outposts of the Spanish Empire in America for the fact that the loss was not so disastrous as was once believed. Reports, petitions, complaints, criminal, civil and ecclesiastical lawsuits, practically anything one can think of, went from the farthest frontiers to Mexico City and often on to Spain — originals, copies, and more copies. Secular and ecclesiastical authorities reviewed them, acted upon them or not, and filed them. Chroniclers used and misused them, then copied from one another, mistakes and all, and sometimes enlarged upon a good story to make two or more better ones.

The regular clergy took great pains to preserve and write the history and achievements of their Orders. In the Franciscan chronicles you will find versions of the history of New Mexico and Texas from their beginnings. One of the most useful is Fray Agustín de Vetancurt's *Teatro Mexicano* (México, 1696; Madrid: Colección Chimalistac, 1960). In the eighteenth century Fray Francisco Antonio de la Rosa Figueroa organized the Archive of the Convento Grande in Mexico City and compiled a *Becerro General* of the friars (MS. in Ayer Collection, Newberry Library, Chicago) adding to, and sometimes correcting Vetancurt. Neither of these men ever visited the far north, but both of them not only had access to the documents but undoubtedly heard some things at first hand from those who returned from the frontier. For eighteenth-century New Mexico, Fray Francisco Atanasio Domínguez's statement of what he found in 1776 is a sad corrective to Benavides's "hopefully exaggerated prospectus" of a century and a half earlier. (Eleanor B. Adams and Fray Angelico Chavez, eds. and trans., *The Missions of New Mexico, 1776,* Albuquerque: The University of New Mexico Press, 1956, 1975.)

Domínguez and his companion, young Fray Silvestre Vélez de Escalante, joined in the search for new routes to establish land communications between the old frontiers of Sonora and New Mexico and the new establishments of upper California. Their goal was Monterey. They did not reach it, but their explorations into Utah from Santa Fe, combined with Fray Francisco Garcés's solitary peregrinations from the Pacific coast to the Hopi pueblos, help to make the year 1776 a landmark in the history of the western United States as well as of the east coast. This was the year that Juan Bautista de Anza was responsible for the founding of the great city of St. Francis by the Golden Gate.

The Spanish authorities believed in the exploration of papers as well as territory, in the usefulness of the recorded experience of earlier pioneers. Although the governor of New Mexico said that his archive contained "nothing but old fragments," Vélez de Escalante assembled from it most of the data concerning New Mexico used by Fray Agustín de Morfi in his works on the northern frontiers. Suffering from chronic ill health and nearing the end of his short but eventful life, this versatile young man compiled an *Extracto de Noticias* which, published in an incomplete and inac-

5

curate version in the mid-nineteenth century, remained for many years a major source for the earlier history of New Mexico.

During the early eighteenth century Jesuit Father Eusebio Francisco Kino had put Pimería Alta on the mission map and recorded the details in his *Favores Celestiales,* rediscovered and published in translation by Herbert E. Bolton in 1919. Other prominent members of the Society of Jesus, such as Francisco Xavier Alegre and José Ortega, carried the story of their *Apostólicos Afanes* through mid-century. The Franciscans from the missionary colleges who continued the work in this area after the Jesuit expulsion in 1767 narrated the vicissitudes of missions and explorations — the indefatigable explorer Fray Francisco Garcés, the keen observer Fray Pedro Font, and the historian Fray Francisco Antonio Barbastro. It was Barbastro who gave Fray Juan Domingo de Arricivita the Sonora material included in Part II of the chronicle of the Colegio de la Santa Cruz of Querétaro, published in 1792. This chronicle, with its earlier part (1746) by Fray Isidro Félix de Espinosa (the biographer of the "North American Pilgrim" Fray Antonio Margil de Jesús) is a primary source for the history of the northern frontier from the Gulf of Mexico to the Gulf of California. Fray Junípero Serra and Fray Francisco Palóu recorded the expansion out of the heartland of the Southwest into California.

Now we come to a new phase in Southwestern historiography. In the late eighteenth century the Spanish government conceived a project for a new general history of the Indies. In response to royal orders an enormous selection of manuscripts was sent to Spain. Many were copies, and there were often several copies of the same items, not always as accurate and complete as we might like. They turn up now in various places, including the National Archive of Mexico, in various repositories in Madrid, in France, England, and the United States. Despite the flaws, for many years they were prime sources. Like the Spanish Archives of New Mexico in the early American period, the documentary records of the viceroyalty suffered during the turbulent years after Mexican independence. Although the National Archive was founded in 1823, corrupt officials abstracted some papers, soldiers destroyed or sold others, and for lack of room many were dispersed and forgotten in various parts of the city. To this day finds continue to be made in unlikely places — one of the things that makes basic research exciting in spite of periods of fruitless drudgery. Although conditions have improved considerably in recent years, and the official work of organization and cataloguing has made great strides, there are places where the work has hardly begun and dusty mountains of disheveled paper await rescue or further decay.

During the nineteenth century the studies of such men as Hubert H. Bancroft, George Parker Winship, Justin Winsor, Woodbury Lowery, and Charles F. Lummis threw new light on Southwestern history. But the golden age of new discoveries of the old began almost seventy years ago. Adolph Bandelier had already made use of original material he found in New Mexico, some of which has disappeared, but it was in the second decade of this century that he began a systematic search in Spanish and Mexican archives which resulted in the collection published by Charles W. Hackett in 1923–1937 under the sonorous title *Historical Documents relating to New Mexico, Nueva Vizcaya, and Approaches thereto, to 1773.* Southwestern scholars owe a great debt to Dr. J. Franklin Jameson, Director of the Division of Historical Research, Carnegie Institution of Washington, who enthusiastically encouraged and supported the new trend. In 1913, also under Carnegie auspices, Herbert E. Bolton's *Guide to the Materials for the History of the United States in the Principal Archives of Mexico* (Washington, D.C., 1913; New York: Kraus Reprint Corporation, 1965) marked the beginning of an era. A few years later Charles E. Chapman's *Catalogue of Materials in the Archivo General de Indias for the History of the West Coast and the American Southwest* (Berkeley: University of California Press, 1919) carried the new guideposts to Spain. Both are still indispensable and they have set the pace for innumerable basic research guides of greater and lesser scope by Mexican, Spanish, and U.S. scholars. Among the early guides we must mention Ralph Emerson Twitchell's calendar, *The Spanish Archives of New Mexico* (2 vols., Cedar Rapids: Torch Press, 1914), not omitting to point out that this work was actually based on the cards made at the Library of Congress by Elizabeth Howard West, who later spent some years in Sevilla collecting material for the Library of Congress.

At the inaugural meeting of the Western History Association in Santa Fe in 1961 France V. Scholes justly attributed the outstanding achievements of the new phase of Southwestern historical scholarship to the wide-ranging archival investigations pioneered by Bolton and Chapman. ("Historiography of the Spanish Southwest: Retrospect and Prospect," in J. Ross Toole et al., eds., *Probing the American West, Papers from the Santa Fe Conference,* Santa Fe: Museum of New Mexico Press, 1962). As Ray Allen Billington has pointed out in his introduction to John Francis Bannon's "golden jubilee" volume, *The Spanish Borderlands Frontier, 1513–1821,* Bolton's labors resulted not only in the imposing corpus of his own works, which range from Georgia to the Pacific Coast, from the sixteenth century to the nineteenth century, but in "the emergence of a new school of histori-

7

cal interpretation. Its concern was with the peopling of the continent, but particularly with the cultural conflicts and adaptations that occurred when two frontiers met as they did in the southwestern United States where the northward-moving Spaniards and the westward-moving Anglo-Americans joined in conflict during the early nineteenth century." Since Bolton published *The Spanish Borderlands* in 1921 not only he and his students, and their students after them, but many other dedicated scholars, have applied themselves to the research needed to solve the problems he stated. Much has been done and much remains to be done.

The new documentation set off lengthy debate (which continues to this day) about the enigmatic Friar Marcos in books and periodicals — and the contenders included Percy M. Baldwin, Carl O. Sauer, Henry R. Wagner, Lansing B. Bloom, and Cleve Hallenbeck. George P. Hammond and Agapito Rey, as well as J. Lloyd Mecham, increased our knowledge of the early expeditions. Bolton's *Coronado* followed the Hammond and Rey publication of the *Narratives* of the expedition. More recently the latter have brought the earlier accounts together in *The Rediscovery of New Mexico* (Albuquerque: The University of New Mexico Press, 1966), while in his annotations to *A Colony on the Move, Gaspar Castaño de Sosa's Journal, 1590–1591* (Santa Fe: The School of American Research, 1965), Albert H. Schroeder has collated documentary and archaeological evidence. By making meticulous textual comparisons Fray Angelico Chavez has cleared up some long-standing misconceptions in *Coronado's Friars* (Washington, D.C.: Academy of American History, 1968). These are merely the highlights of what has been and is being done for the early contact period.

Hammond soon made himself the authority on Oñate. France V. Scholes's studies of seventeenth-century New Mexico, based chiefly on his discoveries in the Mexican National Archive and most of them first published in the *New Mexico Historical Review* over the years from 1928 to 1975, have never been surpassed. Charles W. Hackett and Charmion Clair Shelby gave us the documents for the Pueblo Revolt of 1680. J. Manuel Espinosa is the expert on don Diego de Vargas and the Reconquest.

For eighteenth-century New Mexico no one has yet been able to match the Scholes overall picture of pre-Revolt society. Some of us are working on various topics, but the wealth of source material now readily available, and more is being added all the time, is, as Scholes remarked, "almost embarrassing." Alfred B. Thomas is responsible for a series of important documentary publications on explorations and Indian campaigns. Since 1961 Oakah L. Jones, in *Pueblo Warriors and Spanish Conquest* (Norman: University of Oklahoma Press, 1966) and Ted J. Warner in his article, "Don

8

Féliz Martínez and the Santa Fe Presidio" (*New Mexico Historical Review*, 45:4, 1970), have shed much needed light on specific aspects of military history in New Mexico.

New material on ecclesiastical and mission history continues to fill in the gaps, and the same is true of Indian tribes and relations with them. There are indications that ethnohistory is coming to life again. Jack D. Forbes continues to work along this line. In *The Jicarilla Apaches, a Study in Survival* (DeKalb: Northern Illinois University Press, 1974) Dolores A. Gunnerson revises earlier ideas about the Athapascans. Carroll L. Riley is restudying the early chronicles and raising some questions about accepted interpretations. But we still await a successor to Frederick W. Hodge.

Marc Simmons has published a study of Spanish administration in the late colonial period. Current interest in land tenure and water rights has inspired much documentary research and a few sound treatments of particular cases, along with a good deal of naïve oversimplification. It is high time for wider use of the voluminous legal literature in Spanish on this important topic and more precise understanding of the highly specialized terminology. In this, as in many other fields, it is unwise to be lulled by the comfortable assumption that simple knowledge of Spanish, whether native or acquired in the classroom, is adequate for all purposes.

The material for the beginnings and early history of Texas is scattered, and much of it is included in volumes of wider scope. In addition to Bolton, the great names in the field are those of the Mexican Vito Alessio Robles and the Texas Carlos E. Castañeda. Publication on individual problems in this area continues.

It is almost impossible to treat the early history of Arizona as separate from that of the bordering Mexican state of Sonora. Again Bolton made major contributions, as have the Jesuits Bannon and Peter Masten Dunne. Ernest Burrus, S.J., ably assisted by Charles J. Polzer, S.J., continues to add to the extensive research on Father Kino. The late John Augustine Donohue, S.J., and John L. Kessell have undertaken major research on this region after Kino, some of which has been published.

Chapman and Bolton head the California list. Maynard Geiger, O.F.M., heir to the tradition of Zephyrin Engelhart, is the authority on Fray Junípero Serra and has added greatly to our knowledge of the Franciscan missionary enterprise. Although the roster of historians of California is lengthy and distinguished, and belongs to the Boltonlands, it is on the fringe of the Southwest.

Brief mention must also be made of general works, such as those of Herbert I. Priestley, which serve as indispensable background for regional

9

studies. In 1962 Edward H. Spicer's *Cycles of Conquest* came out. A provocative and ambitious attempt at synthesis, it is flawed by weaknesses in historical fact and bibliography. To interpret the Southwest we must consult the works of J. Lloyd Mecham, Vito Alessio Robles, Philip W. Powell, Max L. Moorhead, the Spaniard Luis Navarro García, and others who have specialized in the history of northern Mexico.

Scholes ("Historiography") has pointed out that the emphasis upon "pure narrative, biography, and the dramatic event" was a natural result of "the discovery and eager exploitation of rich and exciting archival records" — and a worthy one, despite criticism by proponents of a more sophisticated approach. I venture to add that in my opinion sound social and intellectual history cannot be written except on the basis of the spade work in the source materials.

In looking to the future Scholes emphasized the need for continuing interest and support for archival investigation and documentary publication by both public and private institutions. The Academy of American Franciscan History and the Jesuit Historical Institute are in the vanguard. The Universities of Texas and California are adding to their collections. The University of New Mexico, with the nucleus of a magnificent research library of archival sources, owed mainly to the efforts of Scholes, Hammond, and Bloom, has failed to follow up its brilliant start and has added little since the photographing of the New Mexico land grant papers and the publication of *A Guide to the Microfilm of Papers Relating to New Mexico Land Grants* by Albert James Díaz (Albuquerque: University of New Mexico Press, 1960). On the other hand, the State of New Mexico Records Center is doing a remarkable job of making its collections available and searching the highways and byways for more. They have filmed the Archives of the Archdiocese of Santa Fe, earlier organized and calendared by Fray Angelico Chavez (*Archives of the Archdiocese of Santa Fe, 1678–1900,* Washington, D.C.: Academy of American Franciscan History, 1957). They are publishing new guides to their holdings, including the Spanish Archives of New Mexico and the Mexican Archives of New Mexico (*Calendar of the Microfilm Edition of the Spanish Archives of New Mexico, 1621–1821,* Santa Fe, 1968; *Calendar of the Microfilm Edition of the Mexican Archives of New Mexico, 1821–1846,* Santa Fe, 1970). The lion's share of the credit must go to Myra Ellen Jenkins. The Arizona State Historical Society in Tucson is very active. Kieran McCarthy, O.F.M., has made San Xavier del Bac a new center for the study of this region by collecting quantities of primary source material from the archives. Microfilm of the rich archive of Hidalgo del Parral, Chihuahua, earlier saved from oblivion by the late editor of the *Correo del Parral,* José G. Rocha, is now available in various collections. The Centro de Documentación in Mexico City has been photographing local archival material throughout the republic, some of which pertains to our Southwest. And there are other projects too numerous to mention.

Surely professional Southwestern historians may take pride in a very respectable record of sixty-odd years of hard work and achievement. Nevertheless, there are complaints that we have been guilty of serious neglect. Some younger students tell us that they plan to remedy this by tackling "the necessary but herculean task of reportage on primary sources available in the archives." The task is endless and competent recruits are more than welcome. Certainly we shall all be delighted if they fulfill their boast and "become the leading authorities in the near future." As a sample of the problems they may encounter, perhaps not so frequently as before, and of the kind of debt they owe to their predecessors, I should like to tell the story of one collection that might now be dispersed or lost beyond recall had it not been for two archival bloodhounds of an earlier generation, France V. Scholes and the late Lansing B. Bloom.

Scholes made his first trip to Mexico City in 1927. Early in 1928 Fanny Bandelier, Adolph's widow, told him there were said to be New Mexican papers in the Biblioteca Nacional which she had not been allowed to see. Scholes was more successful. Shown to a little room upstairs in the former Augustinian church which still houses the library, he soon saw enough to know that he had struck gold and obtained permission from the Director to mine it. In the short time at his disposal he sorted out some ten bulky *legajos* of New Mexico papers and put them in chronological order. Later in the same year, when they met in Spain, Lansing B. Bloom, editor of the *New Mexico Historical Review,* persuaded Scholes to publish his hasty preliminary list of these documents without delay, in the hope of preventing further neglect or even loss of this important collection (*New Mexico Historical Review,* 3:3, 1928; 4:1, 1929). Then, in the summer of 1930, Scholes made negative photostats for the Library of Congress, positives of which now fill long shelves of hefty volumes at the Bancroft Library, University of California, and the Zimmerman Library, University of New Mexico.

This great find was the Archive of the Franciscan Province of the Holy Gospel of Mexico which contains priceless data on almost all the areas of Franciscan activity in New Spain from the beginning and is very rich indeed in material for the history of the borderlands — and not only ecclesiastical history as some might assume. Here was the complete original of

Vélez de Escalante's *Extracto* (which I have prepared for publication), one of the many items copied in part at the Convento Grande in the late eighteenth century for the use of the new chronicler of the Indies. Father Domínguez's visitation of New Mexico was there. Castañeda later found Morfi's history of Texas. Eighteenth-century archivist Antonio de la Rosa Figueroa's catalogue contains sometimes mordant critical comments on people and papers. His system can now be followed but was not immediately apparent in the disorder when the papers were discovered. The Biblioteca Nacional has since made its own chronological catalogue by areas, and in all but a few cases it is now possible to collate the various listings of one of its most important treasures.

Present-day Southwestern historians are the heirs to a fine tradition of honest scholarship which we should do our best to perpetuate, remembering that we are historians, that history demands its own rational approach, and that in the long run we shall best perform our proper service by doing our own thing in our own way.

*Bibliographical Note:*

With the aid of the following references the interested reader should be able to locate data on specific topics, personalities, and publications mentioned briefly above.

The most comprehensive archival guide is Lino Gómez Canedo, O.F.M., *Los archivos de la historia de América Período colonial español,* 2 vols., México, D.F., 1961. Volume 1 covers the archives and libraries of Spain and Spanish America; volume 2, those of the United States and Europe (except Spain). Gómez Canedo's notes cite many previous catalogues and guides. The Bancroft Library, University of California, Berkeley, has photographed the material listed in Chapman's *Catalogue* and collated the older numbers he used with the present cataloguing system of the Archivo General de las Indias, Sevilla. Although it is directed toward students of Mexican history, *Research in Mexican History, Topics, Methodology, Sources, and a Practical Guide to Field Research,* edited by Richard E. Greenleaf and Michael C. Meyer (Lincoln: University of Nebraska Press, 1973) is an up-to-date vade mecum which should be equally useful to researchers of the documentary history of the Spanish Southwest.

*The Spanish Southwest, 1542–1794,* by Henry R. Wagner (The Quivira Society, 1937, republished by Arno Press, New York, 1967), with its critical annotations, remains the outstanding publication of its kind. For a comparatively recent summary of pertinent publications, including articles, see John Francis Bannon, *The Spanish Borderlands Frontier, 1513–1821* (Albuquerque: University of New Mexico Press, 1974), pp. 257–87. The *Handbook of Latin American Studies* (Cambridge, Mass.: Harvard University Press; Gainesville, Fla.: University of Florida Press, 1936–) includes publications on the Spanish Southwest and is helpful in keeping abreast of current research.

# AUTHORS AND BOOKS
# IN COLONIAL NEW MEXICO

*Marc Simmons*

∴ઝઈ∴

SOME YEARS AGO, a deer hunter, seeking shelter from a storm, entered a shallow cave in the Ladrón Mountains west of Socorro, New Mexico. Back in one corner, almost buried under sand and fallen rock, he discovered something that made him forget all about hunting. It was a small trove of relics — articles once owned by Spaniards who had explored and settled the Rio Grande Valley centuries before. There was a steel helmet, a sword, and a hide trunk filled with books. Gathering up the bonanza, the lucky hunter hiked back to his pickup and headed for home.

For a princely sum, he sold the helmet to an antique dealer. The sword came to rest over his mantelpiece. And the books?

The books, with their cracked bindings and frazzled pages, seemed to be of no interest or value, written as they were in some strange language which the finder failed to recognize. Since it was inconceivable that such trifles could be converted to cash, the little library was carted off to the dump, while the trunk that had once protected it ended up in a garage as a catch-all for worn-out spark plugs and greasy nuts and bolts.

If those books could have found their way into appreciative and intelligent hands, without a doubt they would have added something to our small fund of knowledge about the reading habits of colonial New Mexicans. For two-and-a-half centuries, Spanish New Mexico was a raw and thinly populated frontier where books of any kind were a rarity. Those few and treasured volumes that did manage to travel up the Camino Real from Mexico

City, Zacatecas, Durango, and Chihuahua to the libraries of governors and missionaries had a rough time of it, for weather and insects, floods, Indian raids, and simple human neglect took their toll. It was perhaps an Apache raiding party that carried the helmet, the sword, and the book-filled trunk to the cave in the Ladróns where our jet-age hunter stumbled upon them. Had he but known it, books dating from New Mexico's colonial period are far more scarce than armor or weapons, and, to some persons at least, are far more valuable.

Who bears the honor of having brought the first book northward out of New Spain to the wide and sun-splashed land of New Mexico? A likely candidate is the priest, Fray Marcos de Niza, the man sent to the far frontier by Viceroy Antonio de Mendoza in 1539 for the purpose of confirming rumors of seven golden cities. We know from his own account that Fray Marcos traveled light as he moved with his Indian escort up the west side of Mexico, through southern Arizona, and to within sight of the southernmost of the Zuñi pueblos. A safe guess would be that he found room among his few personal articles for at least a breviary, the small liturgical book containing prayers, psalms, and other readings which all priests are obliged to recite daily. Missals and books of devotion must certainly have found a place in the baggage of the five friars accompanying the Coronado expedition to New Mexico in 1540. So it is reasonable to assume that the first printed volume ever opened and read under New Mexico's shining, turquoise sky was one of sacred content; and, in fact, all evidence available suggests that throughout Spanish times, the majority of books brought here pertained to religion.

Juan de Oñate, member of a prominent Zacatecas mining family, led the first colonizing expedition to the upper Rio Grande in 1598. Before departure for the north, the royal inspector, Juan de Frías Salazar, conducted a meticulous inspection of all the material goods assembled by Oñate and his settlers for their use in the new country. The list Salazar prepared as part of the official record provides our best glimpse of what provisions sixteenth-century Spaniards considered necessary and useful for a pioneering project. Food, livestock, weapons and gunpowder, tools and hardware, clothing, trade goods, medicines, and church furnishings are counted in abundance. Included among the necessities is a staggering sum of more than one hundred thousand horseshoe nails. Yet, in all this enumeration, books rarely receive mention.

Nevertheless, at least one bibliophile did participate in the expedition: Captain Alonso de Quesada, who, by coincidence, bore the same name as Cervantes's fictional knight-errant before he assumed the title of Don Quixote. The Salazar inventory indicates that Captain Quesada conveyed to the land of the Pueblos, "seven books, religious and non-religious."[1] Unfortunately, for those of us with curiosity almost four hundred years later, the inspector neglected to include the titles.

Another man with Oñate who added books to his traveling pack was a jack-of-several-trades named Juan del Caso Baraona. The list of arms, tools, and sundry articles he took suggests that he was not only a soldier but a blacksmith and farrier, armorer, gunsmith, and a barber-surgeon. Into his bag of medications and surgical instruments he slipped "five medical books by recognized authorities."[2] His small collection of volumes probably represents the first medical library imported into any part of the present United States.

The possessions — arms, horse equipment, and clothing — listed for still another soldier, Captain Gaspar Pérez de Villagrá, give no hint that he had a passion for letters or that he was destined to become the author of America's earliest epic poem. Born in Spain and graduated from the prestigious University of Salamanca in 1580, Villagrá spent seven years at the court of Philip II before coming to the New World to join in the project for settling New Mexico. His *Historia de la Nueva México,* written in blank verse and published in Alcalá de Henares, Spain, in the year 1610, tells of the slow, painful journey of Oñate's colonists up the Rio Grande, the founding of a first capital at San Juan Pueblo, and the bloody war waged against the Acoma Indians.

A summary judgment of Villagrá's work has been given us by one of the Southwest's pioneer scholars, Adolph F. Bandelier. Sympathetic to its merits and conscious of its obvious shortcomings, he wrote, near the end of the last century: "The book contains very heavy, nay clumsy, poetry. Still it is exceedingly valuable. Villagrá was an execrable poet, but a reliable historian so far as he saw and took part in the events himself. His narration of the tragedy at Acoma and of the recapture of the pueblo is too Homeric altogether; but in this he followed the style of the period."[3]

The high drama attending the conquest of New Mexico surely inspired Captain Villagrá to write his epic, and it is apparent, as Bandelier suggests, that he was influenced also by authors of antiquity who struck the heroic note. His verses are larded with references lifted from the classics — a common practice at which Cervantes pokes fun in his preface to *Don Quixote.* By way of ready illustration, we need only cite the opening words of the first Canto which Villagrá borrowed with little alteration from the *Aeneid.* As if recognizing the limitation of his own poetic gifts, the writer concludes his verses with the admission that, since by profession he is a sword-carrying soldier, he finds "the pen a new and strange implement to wield."[4] This might account for his heavy reliance upon accepted authors, even apart from the fact that the style of the day required it.

We can assume with some confidence that another influence upon Villagrá was Alonso de Ercilla's *La Araucana,* which describes the conflict between Spaniards and Araucanian Indians in Chile during the middle of the sixteenth century. This lofty poem is often acclaimed as the finest heroic verse in the Spanish language. While Villagrá's *Historia* is far less imaginative and less skillfully crafted than *La Araucana,* the two works show a strong similarity in their muscular, American themes and particularly in their charitable attitude toward the Indian. Indeed, both were among the first literary pieces to introduce Europeans to the concept of the "noble savage."

How soon after its publication in 1610 a copy of the *Historia* reached New Mexico we cannot say. Governor Diego de Peñalosa, who assumed office in 1661, had one in his personal library, but likely a copy had been taken to the valley of the Rio Grande even earlier by some official or missionary. Strangely, Villagrá's work later was almost forgotten, in spite of its value as a prime historical source. Many of the colorful details surrounding Spanish exploration and settlement, of which the author took note, appear in no other documents of the Oñate years.

Bandelier discovered the *Historia* when he was doing research at Mexico's National Museum in the early 1890s. For him, it was an eye opener, filling in what was then a yawning gap in the early history of New Mexico. In his customary painstaking manner, he twice transcribed the entire work by hand. One of his copies later went to Harvard's Peabody Museum; the other, "with all the curious 'tail-pieces' and illuminated initial lettering which Bandelier reproduced in watercolor" was given to New Mexico's Senator Thomas B. Catron.[5] In 1933 the Quivira Society issued an English prose edition of Villagrá's epic, prepared by Gilberto Espinosa, thus insuring the work's recogniiton as part of the State's literary legacy from the colonial period.

Captain Villagrá's piece of writing must be regarded as something of an anomaly, for certainly nothing quite like it ever flowed again from the quill of a Spanish New Mexican. The colonists who braved this difficult and often dangerous land seemed disinclined to allocate the time or energy authorship demands, and we look in vain for signs of creative endeavor in the literary arts. This is scarcely surprising since, by any standard, the colonial New Mexicans led an impoverished intellectual life. They never had a printing press, nor more than a handful of books; schools were practically

"Captain Don Gaspar de Villagra, 55 years of age"
from his *Historia de Nueva Mexico* (1610)

non-existent, and the majority of the common people were illiterate. If any man suffered that well-known "hunger in the head," he had little hope of satisfying his craving on this isolated frontier.

The discovery, exploration, and settlement of New Mexico called forth a significant body of writing, but one consisting mainly of chronicles of exploration, government reports and letters, and church documents. It seems that those few colonial citizens who possessed some facility with a pen used it almost exclusively to do their duty by church and state, seldom straying into the creative field of belles-lettres. The priority given to record-keeping grew in part from the Spaniards' penchant for adhering to proper legal forms, and in part from his rigid political and ecclesiastical systems which demanded strict attention to small details. In such writing, there is much to inform but little to excite the imagination. That personal touch that imparts inner warmth is missing.

The explorers' chronicles, enlivened by first-hand impressions of the Southwest's singular landscape and native people, and salted with adventurous episodes, are most apt to engage the attention of modern readers. Even so, they remain of more interest to the historian than to the student of literature. One of the earliest and most popular chronicles in Cabeza de Vaca's *Naufragos,* first published in 1542 and reprinted many times in both Spanish and English. It recounts the author's shipwreck on the Texas coast in 1528 and his seven years of wandering with three companions through the heart of the Spanish borderlands. Whether Cabeza de Vaca actually set foot within the present boundaries of New Mexico is a point still argued by scholars, but there is no doubt that it was his vivid eye-witness report that sparked the journeys of Fray Marcos de Niza and Francisco Vásquez de Coronado and led to the discovery of the fascinating country of the Pueblos.

"He who does not venture forth does not cross the sea," goes the ancient proverb known well to Coronado and to his successors on the New Mexico trail: Rodriguez, Espejo, Castaño de Sosa, and Oñate. All of these stalwart sons of Spain left us full chronicles of their adventuring, and these compose a rich body of historical literature. In them, the reader of today not only can discern the spirit of an age that developed on a truly heroic scale but can glimpse the customs and habits of mind that governed the lives of both Spaniards and Indians in those remote times. Happily, the sixteenth-century narratives are readily accessible in a series of volumes, edited and translated by the able team of George P. Hammond and Agapito Rey.[6]

The writings of Franciscan friars compose another category of colonial literature. Here we would perhaps expect to find only works of colorless and parochial character, but, in fact, amid the plethora of tedious scratchings, there occasionally will surface examples of lively prose. In both the seventeenth and eighteenth centuries, several clerics of keen observation and lively mind prepared official reports on the state of the missions, in which they made illuminating asides on geography, flora and fauna, native customs, economic conditions, and the social and political life of the colonists. Not only do their words provide engaging reading, but they frequently offer historical detail and insight available from no other sources.

Father Alonso de Benavides, who served as custodian or director of the Rio Grande missions from 1622 to 1629, composed the most-quoted and surely the best of these ecclesiastical reports. His *Memorial* on New Mexico was published in Madrid in 1630; and, according to his own statement, four hundred copies were distributed.[7] Within four years, it had been translated and printed in Latin, French, German, and Dutch. Charles F. Lummis published the first English version serially in his periodical *Land of Sunshine,* 1900 to 1901, and he later assisted Frederick W. Hodge in editing a new translation prepared by Mrs. Edward E. Ayer, a volume which was privately printed in 1916 at Chicago.

In Spain, a "memorial" was a summary statement describing a particular event or geographical region, often containing some form of petition addressed to the king or some other important personage. Usually it was printed in a very small edition, intended for limited distribution to officials rather than to the public. Benavides' own *Memorial* was designed to impress the sovereign with the importance of New Mexico as a missionary field and to win for it certain royal favors, namely an appropriation of additional funds for new churches and priests and elevation of the province to the status of a bishopric. In short, the good Father was a promoter, a visionary, who hoped to further the Franciscan cause along the banks of the Rio Grande, and, at the same time, advance his own prospects. He dearly aspired to the honor of being New Mexico's first bishop. In this he was doomed to frustration, for civil authorities in Mexico opposed any change in the province's ecclesiastical status.

There is much of the epic and the miraculous in the Benavides *Memorial* of 1630.[8] Of the brave and nobly inspired citizens of Santa Fe, for example, he says with enthusiasm: "Though they are few and ill-equipped, God hath permitted that they should always come out victorious; and hath caused among the Indians so great a fear of them and of their arquebuses that with only hearing it said that a Spaniard is going to their pueblos, they flee." And these citizens, he continues, are "a folk so punctual in obedience to its governors that to whatever fracas comes up they sally with their weapons and horses at their own cost and do valorous deeds."[9]

19

Miracles were much on the minds of New Mexico's pious friars and they kept constant watch for signs of direct intervention by the Almighty in the serious matter of converting the heathen tribes. With disarming simplicity and perfect faith, Benavides tells of the Hopi accepting Christianity upon witnessing a blind boy gain his sight when a priest touched his eyes with the cross, and he relates the story of a Taos witch struck dead by a thunderbolt for preaching against monogamous marriage. But the divine wonder that beguiled him most, and to which he devotes greatest attention in his *Memorial,* concerned the career of the 29-year-old Mother María de Jesús de Agreda, abbess of a convent in Spain, who claimed to have made "spiritual flights" to New Mexico for the purpose of instructing the Indians in the true faith. Father Benavides satisfied himself as to the validity of this miracle through testimony of native people who claimed to have been visited by a young and beautiful nun, and through a personal interview later with the abbess herself in Spain.

It is worthy of note that this woman not only claimed to have made extraordinary flights to tribes in Arizona and Texas — as well as New Mexico — but she also was the author of a ponderous three-volume life of the Virgin Mary, titled *Mística Cuidad de Dios,* first published in 1670. New Mexico's reconquistador, Don Diego de Vargas, had a copy of the work in his library when he died in 1704, and the first Archbishop of Santa Fe, Jean B. Lamy, possessed a seven-volume edition dating from 1758.[10]

Fray Estévan de Perea, Benavides' successor as custodian of the New Mexican missions, prepared his own two-part study of church affairs. This was printed in Spain in 1632 and 1633 under the title *Truthful Report of the Magnificent Conversion Which Has Been Had in New Mexico.*[11] But neither it nor any other work produced by a Franciscan prior to the Pueblo revolt of 1680 approached the Benavides *Memorial* in richness of detail or in zealous advocacy of the missionary program. Indeed, a century and a half passed before another priest in New Mexico emerged with a gift of writing equal to that of Father Benavides. He was Fray Francisco Atanasio Domínguez.

In 1775, Father Domínguez was sent as canonical visitor to inspect the condition of New Mexico's missions, and also was to undertake the search for a route that would link Santa Fe with the new settlements in California. The latter task he attempted in the company of Fray Silvestre Vélez de Escalante, a young missionary stationed at Zuñi Pueblo. The two men, with a small escort, spent the latter part of 1776 exploring the mountains and canyonlands of Utah, but early snows prevented them from continuing on to California. Back in New Mexico, Domínguez resumed his examination of mission parishes, work which he had interrupted to make the western trip.

During a fourteen-month tour, he looked closely not only at the Church and its work but also at the land and people. Much he found in New Mexico to criticize: missions in disrepair, with their furnishings gone to ruin; clergy and laymen in dire need of discipline; and rude customs which distressed his sense of propriety. Severest condemnation he reserved for the Pueblo Indians and their ways: "To eat their ordinary coarse hash, many (without regard for persons) gather around the bowl or trough and put their filthy hands in it, and so they eat in brotherly fashion and without disgust, although there may be nastiness. Their only napkin for wiping themselves is to shake their hands right over the bowl."[12]

Father Domínguez put into a lengthy manuscript all that he observed and did and delivered it to his religious superiors in Mexico City. They evidently found some of his harsh judgments and forthright comments distasteful, for a note was appended to his document declaring in part, ". . . it lacks proportion, and offers little to the discriminating taste."[13] Then, unlike the *Memorial* of Father Benavides, which had gone to the printers soon after its completion, Domínguez's own extensive report was filed away and forgotten.

No one took notice of it for another one hundred and fifty years. The manuscript seems to have been removed from its dusty sepulcher in the Franciscan archives in Mexico City sometime during the nineteenth century on one of the several occasions when the government confiscated monastic libraries. Eventually it reached a back room of the National Library where *legajos* or bundles of manuscripts were carelessly heaped.

Late in 1927, a young, Harvard-trained historian, France V. Scholes, was working in Mexico City collecting material on colonial New Mexico. From Mrs. Adolph Bandelier, he learned of some heretofore unknown documents in the National Library pertaining to the missionary program in the Southwest. Scholes recognized, after a hurried inspection, that the assorted papers offered important new information not only on church affairs but on Mexico's political administration and Indian warfare during the seventeenth and eighteenth centuries. From this preliminary examination, he prepared a brief calendar which was published the following year in the *New Mexico Historical Review*. One of his entries under Legajo 10 read, "1777. *Visita* and description of New Mexico. The author was probably Fray Domínguez. 135 ff."[14]

The original documents from Mexico's National Library were photographed for the Library of Congress in 1930. Photocopies were later deposited in the special collections of the University of New Mexico Library. Thus, more than a century and a half after the original survey of the Rio Grande missions, a copy of Father Domínguez's report became available to New Mexicans, although it still lacked that special mark of distinction which only publication can provide.

During the 1940s, two persons began to work independently upon a translation of the Domínguez manuscript. One was Eleanor B. Adams, a noted historian and paleographer with the University of New Mexico; the other was Fray Angelico Chavez, a native-born New Mexican and Franciscan priest who had already gained a reputation as a regional poet and novelist. The two agreed to join forces and produce for publication a heavily annotated translation of the mission report, together with ancillary documents illuminating the career of Father Domínguez and of Father Escalante, his companion on the now-well-publicized trip to Utah.

Appropriately, the University of New Mexico Press, under its able director, Roland F. Dickey, elected to publish the work, giving it a handsome format with an eighteenth-century flavor. While the book was in production, Fray Angelico made an important discovery. Cataloging the archives of the Archdiocese of Santa Fe, he turned up an inventory (dated 1788) of the old Franciscan library and archive at Santa Domingo Pueblo, most of which had been destroyed in a calamitous flood in 1886. Father Domínguez himself had inspected the library in 1776 and had prepared a hasty listing of its contents to accompany his report. The two lists were now handed to Miss Adams, an authority on Spanish colonial libraries, for analysis and comparison; and, insofar as possible, she identified each book, giving full title, author, and date of publication. Delighted to hold up publication of the Domínguez book so that the study could be included, Editor Dickey commented: "This Scotland Yard assignment resulted in a list that offered important new perspectives on the status of New Mexico's learning and culture in the seventeen hundreds."[15]

When Domínguez visited the library on his tour, he found two hundred and fifty-six items, including duplicates, many of which showed hard use. The catalog of 1788 found by Fray Angelico listed three hundred and eighty-four entries. These books had apparently been collected in haphazard fashion: some donated by laymen or friars; others contributed by the Franciscan Order; and a few, particularly liturgical works, were supplied by the king. Most, as we would expect, were of a devotional nature, such as prayers, catechisms and sermons, or pertained to the larger category of religious literature, such as homiletic writings by saints or the Church Fathers, theological treatises, canon law, and ecclesiastical history. But there were some titles of secular character, works on civil law, histories of the Spanish Indies, Latin classics (Vergil and Ovid were there), Greek grammars, and a single copy of Antonio de Nebrija's renowned dictionary, first published at Salamanca in 1492. Domínguez observed with some perturbation that certain volumes were missing from the convent library, so he gave instructions prohibiting the mission fathers from taking books without properly signing them out.[16]

The Domínguez report, supported by Adams's analysis of the Franciscan library and archive and by other pertinent material, and decorated with line drawings of the provincial churches as they probably looked in the latter eighteenth century, finally appeared as a comely book in 1956 under the title of *The Missions of New Mexico, 1776*. Within a few years the edition was exhausted, and copies brought upward of $75 on the used book market. Then, in 1975, the State of New Mexico sponsored a second printing as part of its contribution to the Bicentennial celebration.

One can only speculate as to Father Domínguez's reaction had he been able to peer into the future and perceive that the manuscript into which he poured such effort would one day be published — not in the language in which he wrote but in that of Spain's great enemy, England. He would have experienced profound surprise to learn that his work, in its second printing, would lend honor to the founding of the American nation. It remains one of the many infelicities of history that Fray Francisco Atanasio Domínguez died with no inkling of the strange manner in which recognition would at last be accorded him. Could he but have had a vision of the beautiful book New Mexicans were destined to make of his manuscript, we may assume that the humble padre would have been pardonably pleased.

Apart from official church reports, like those of Benavides and Domínguez, one other class of works by the missionary fathers, the dictionaries and grammars of Indian languages, particularly interests the historian and bibliographer. Vocabularies and devotional tracts in Nahuatl, the idiom of the Aztecs, were among the first books printed in Mexico City. There was strong sentiment among the Mexican clergy in favor of making Nahuatl the official Indian language for all New Spain, since it was easily taught and learned; and, according to one friar, commenting in 1550, it seemed "an extremely elegant tongue, as elegant as any in the world."[17] This partiality for Nahuatl by the missionaries perhaps explains why half a dozen or so books in that language were included in the collection of New Mexico's Franciscan library at Santo Domingo Pueblo.

When priests first began their herculean efforts to convert the Indians of central Mexico, they learned Nahuatl as well as the languages of lesser tribes, and in them produced an amazing diversity of religious literature. Their example should have inspired the early missionaries in New Mexico to pursue linguistic studies, for here the need was obvious. The Pueblos spoke four distinct languages, and the nomad people still others. Yet, the records tell us that the padres seldom mastered the local tongue, nor did they have much success in teaching their neophytes Spanish. Even in such important matters as the delivery of sermons and the hearing of confessions, they depended upon very imperfect interpreters.

The only friar in New Mexico, who we know for a certainty attempted to carry on the tradition of the early Nahuatl scholars, was Father Géronimo Zárate Salmerón, a contemporary of Benavides. He is credited with converting the people of Jemez Pueblo, building the first church there and writing a *Doctrina,* or catechism, in the Jemez language.[18] His contemporaries reported that he was both an accomplished linguist and an exemplary priest. Unfortunately, no trace of his *Doctrina* has ever been found, leading us to believe that it was destroyed, along with most other documents in the province, during the Pueblo revolt of 1680.

In the matter of colonial writing, one author, Pedro Bautista Pino, stands alone with a unique work at the end of the Spanish period, just as Pérez de Villagrá stood by himself at the beginning. Pino, a prominent businessman and for a time *alcalde,* or magistrate, of the city of Santa Fe, was elected in 1810 as New Mexico's first, and only, representative to the Spanish cortes, or parliament. He went to Cádiz in southern Spain, where the cortes had fled to escape Napoleon's forces, and there composed a lengthy treatise intended to acquaint his fellow parliamentarians with New Mexico's condition and needs. His effort was published in 1812, a forty-eight-page volume, octavo, entitled *Exposición sucinta y sencilla de a provincia del Nuevo México.* In a straightforward, unvarnished manner, Pino presented a detailed description of his homeland's history, geography, people, politics, and economy, giving a full and clear picture of provincial life in the years just before independence. The book, translated in English and published by the Quivira Society in 1942, is one of the indispensable items in any collection of New Mexicana.[19]

One curious twist about the writing of the *Exposición* is it appears that Pino, handicapped by the rudimentary education available to him in New Mexico, sought assistance in the phrasing of his book. He, of course, furnished the basic information and probably wrote a rough first draft; but it was left to another to provide the final polish and ready the manuscript for the printers. The ghost or editor, a clever fellow who took pride in his work, was unwilling to remain entirely anonymous. So, in the course of the text, he entered his full name in an acrostic. The initial letter beginning each sentence, except the first, in the section treating "Gifts presented to hostile Indians," taken together, spell out Juan López Cancelada, the name of a well-known author and editor. Hubert Howe Bancroft first called attention to the small trick in a note on the *Exposición* in his *History of Arizona and New Mexico,* 1889. In catching it, he, or one of his paid researchers, must be rated the equal of Sherlock Holmes.

It is of some interest that the city of Cádiz held special ceremonies on October 12, 1975, to honor the participation of Pedro Pino in the Spanish cortes. Two of his descendants from Santa Fe presented a commemorative plaque to the city fathers, along with a copy of the English edition of the *Exposición.* In that small event, a historical circle was completed, and Don Pedro received a belated thanks from the mother country for his able representation of a distant corner of the empire.

References to books belonging to private individuals in colonial New Mexico are few and scattered, but those we do have offer valuable insights on the quality of provincial life. Since the majority of the population was unlettered, circulation of the meager stock of books was restricted almost entirely to governors and their families, a handful of the most prominent citizens, and the clergy. Members of this elite fraternity of readers loaned their treasured volumes to one another, and doubtless, in discussions, exchanged ideas developed from them.

One person who made use of the books at hand for political purposes was Father Juan de Vidania. Historians regard him as an intemperate and self-serving priest who took the side of Governor Luís de Rosas (1637–1641) in that official's violent quarrel with the Franciscans. The controversy arose over questions of ecclesiastical privilege and the extent of the Governor's jurisdiction with regard to activities of the missionaries. It was a perennial problem in seventeenth-century New Mexico; and, at the height of the friction under Rosas, the province split into warring camps. Because he supported the Governor and served as his closest advisor, Vidania was denounced by his fellow friars as a rascal and a traitor. Specifically, they attacked his bending of ecclesiastical law, declaring that his interpretations were so erroneous and improper that he was unfit to read Scripture and the canons.[20]

In a series of opinions and letters — drafted at the request of Rosas — Father Vidania formulated arguments and presented justifications for his patron's high-handed policies toward the clergy. In these, he leaned heavily on both secular and ecclesiastical authorities, citing classical authors, law books, decrees of the Council of Trent, and papal bulls. In numerous instances, his opinions are buttressed with verbatim quotations from such sources as Caesar's *Gallic Wars,* Aristotle's *Topics,* Ovid's *Metamorphoses,* and the works of St. Augustine and St. Thomas Aquinas. Evidently these books existed either in the library of the Governor's Palace or in that of the Santa Fe rectory.[21] In the end, Vidania's many learnéd references failed him, for both he and the Governor suffered disgrace and punishment.

Two of Rosas's successors, Bernardo López de Mendizábal (1659–1691) and Diego de Peñalosa (1661–1664), each had serious altercations with the missionaries and each suffered arrest and trial by the Inquisition. Their misfortune proves a boon for historians interested in colonial culture, because the Inquisition court records contain a number of inventories of personal property, including a miscellany of books confiscated by the authorities. Indeed, one suspicious volume in Italian was used as evidence against Governor López's wife, Doña Teresa de Aguilera, who was also brought to trial by the ecclesiastical body.

López was a well-educated man for his day, having studied arts and canon law at the Royal and Pontifical University in Mexico City. Doña Teresa, of an Italian father and an Irish mother, had been raised in an aristocratic household in Spain; and, like her husband, was a cultured person accustomed to courtly amenities. The pair, disdainful of frontier folk and their rustic ways, did not fare well in the rough-and-tumble provincial capital of Santa Fe, and neighbors and servants alike found plenty of harsh words to raise against them. Their apparent neglect of religious duties and some strange quirks of behavior led gossipmongers to whisper that they were practicing Jews, or perhaps heretics. López further antagonized many New Mexicans by his harsh treatment of the Franciscans, so it came as no surprise that, at the conclusion of his term, an order arrived from Mexico City for his arrest as well as that of his wife.

The contents of the López library was heavily weighted, as we would expect, with religious literature, but it also included a significant body of secular non-fiction, belles-lettres, and works in technical fields. For light reading, López possessed a copy of *Don Quixote,* an original edition of Villagrá's *Historia de la Nueva Mexico,* and an unidentified volume of *Comedias,* or plays, by different authors. It was another work in this category, *Orlando Furioso,* by the Italian Ludovico Ariosto, that produced trouble for Doña Teresa. This book, an innocuous epic poem, enjoyed immense popularity at the time and influenced many writers of Spain's Golden Age. But the country-bumpkins in Santa Fe had never heard of it; all they knew was that the Governor's haughty lady appeared to derive a great deal of pleasure from a book set down in an odd tongue. She freely explained that it was written in Italian and concerned love, and that it had been given to her by her father. Yet the petty folk professed to believe that it contained "English heresies," and hence they concluded that Doña Teresa herself must be a heretic.

To this charge, as well as others, Doña Teresa prepared a reply after she and her husband had been returned to Mexico City for formal indictment. Her explanation was simple. Having been born in Italy and learning Italian as her first tongue, she did not want to forget it, and that that was the sole reason she took pleasure in reading *Orlando Furioso*.[22] In her defense, she declared: "The said book contains nothing against our Holy Faith but only what the books called romances of chivalry usually contain: enchantments and wars." And later, she added, "If the book had been evil, [my father] would not have permitted me to read it, nor would he have done so, for he was a very good Christian. And this book, according to what I heard from him and other persons, has been translated into our Castilian language, like the Petrarch, of which it is a companion volume although the style is different."[23]

Doña Teresa's explanation evidently was not wholly acceptable to the Inquisitors, for they remained perplexed as to why she was not content to read "ordinary books in the Castillian language."[24] Nevertheless, at the conclusion of proceedings extending over two years, the court suspended her case for lack of evidence that she was either a heretic or a practicing Jew. The poor woman had already spent some twenty months in jail, but the relief at being freed prompted her to "give great thanks to God Our Lord and to this Holy Tribunal."[25] Her husband, Don Bernardo, had no share in her good fortune; death had claimed him in the dungeons before the Inquisitors could decide his fate.

Don Diego de Peñalosa, who followed López as Governor of New Mexico, ran into his own problems with the ecclesiastical and civil authorities. In 1644, he was suspended from office, in part for making scurrilous remarks regarding the provincial head of the Franciscan Order and the Holy Office of the Inquisition. He left Santa Fe and returned to Mexico City, taking with him a portion of his large library. There he was arrested, his property was placed under embargo, and detailed inventories were made of all possessions, including his books. Peñalosa's collection, like that of his predecesor, López, was dominated by devotional works; but there was also a variety of volumes on political philosophy, history, theology, law, and even a treatise on horsemanship. He also had a few novels, a book of plays, and a copy of Villagrá's *Historia de la Nueva México*.

Evidence suggests that the hapless Peñalosa had indulged in the reading of forbidden books, for, while he was in jail awaiting trial, the Inquisitors pointedly informed him that he should have avoided "papers or books that did not carry the approval of the Holy Mother Church, the place where they were written or printed, the name of the printer or scribe, the author's name, and authorization."[26] This earlier lapse made it difficult for the ex-governor to obtain reading matter to while away his prison hours; his petitions for books were repeatedly denied, including a request for a Spanish translation of Count Mayolino Bisaccioni's *Civil Wars of England* (published 1658). Finally, the Inquisition took pity on him and permitted the delivery of an appropriate "spiritual book." But the court showed little leniency when it handed down a decision on Peñalosa's case. He was subjected to a heavy fine and perpetually banished from New Spain and the West Indies.

The difficulties experienced by Governor López de Mendizábal and Peñalosa with the Inquisition point up the problems faced by Spanish colonial citizens when their reading tastes — indeed, when any of their daily activities — appeared to stray toward some path not strictly orthodox. The line separating what was allowed from what was prohibited was drawn so thin that persons with an innocent fancy for polite letters or with a grain of intellectual curiosity could easily slip into dangerous shallows almost before they were aware of it.

The problem could become particularly acute when it involved books of esoteric knowledge, especially those on astrology. One branch of this pseudo-science enjoyed formal acceptance, as suggested by the fact that in colonial times the University of Mexico's Chair of Mathematics included, under its wing, instruction in astrology as an aid to the compilation of almanacs. Don Carlos de Sigüenza y Góngora, an outstanding scholar who assumed the Chair in 1672, put no stock in the subject at all, a stand which brought him into conflict with many learnéd professors. When he wrote a vigorously worded pamphlet designed to show that comets were not warnings from God of coming disaster, as most astrologers claimed, he was taken to task by none other than Father Eusebio Kino, who was then in Mexico City preparing to undertake his missionary labors on the northern frontier.[27]

Concerning the falsehood of one phase of astrology, however, there existed almost universal agreement. This was the activity known as "judiciary" astrology which involved the reading of the future in the stars or casting of horoscopes. The Inquisition, in a strongly phrased edict issued in 1616, denounced the practice and imposed stern penalties. "There is no human art or science," it declared, "capable of manifesting the things which are to come when they are dependent on the will of man, for this has been reserved by God our Lord for Himself, with His eternal wisdom."[28] Still many persons were incapable of determining which parts of astrology were permissible.

How many people in colonial New Mexico, fascinated by the arcane arts, went delving into forbidden astrological practices cannot be known. It was shown at the trial of Governor López's wife that she owned and often consulted certain almanacs, but this fact was not taken as proof of any clandestine interest in horoscopes.

In 1626 when Father Alonso de Benavides was investigating the prevalence of superstition along the Rio Grande, he took testimony from a citizen, Lucas de Figueroa, regarding a suspicious volume on astrology. Figueroa stated that once, while visiting in the house of a Mexican Indian living in Santa Fe, he had found there a curious book describing the character of persons born under each planet, and foretelling future events in their lives and their hour of death. Since the Indian could not read, the witness asked to borrow it, and, taking it to his home, he proceeded to cast horoscopes. After several months, a Franciscan lay-brother came, claimed the book was his, and carried it off. In relating the incident, Figueroa became aware he had trod on dangerous ground. So he closed his testimony by professing that his activities had been undertaken solely for amusement; he understood perfectly that no one could predict the future and that all things were subject to the will of God. Benavides, more broad-minded than many clerics of his day, apparently accepted the explanation and dismissed the episode.[29]

In New Mexico, the agent of the Inquisition — usually one of the Franciscan friars acting under special commission — kept watch for any titles listed on the Church's *Index of Prohibited Books,* a compilation first drawn up in 1559 and revised periodically thereafter. But admittedly with the scarcity of books on the frontier, the censor seldom had to exercise his oppressive function.

As the power of the Inquisition waned toward the end of the colonial period, civil officials took on the job of curbing the circulation of undesirable reading matter both as it pertained to public faith and morals and to revolutionary political ideas. In the Spanish Archives, preserved today in Santa Fe, can be found a number of decrees, some by the King himself, others by viceregal officials, requiring the Governor of New Mexico to search for and confiscate specific inflammatory books. One of these concerns a curious work entitled *The Year 2044,* written anonymously in French and published in London in 1776. The governor was advised that this pernicious volume "promoted liberty" and looked to the destruction of the Catholic religion and the Spanish empire. For the public good, he was instructed to seize and burn any copies that might have slipped into the New Mexican settlements.[30]

An equally harsh decree reached Santa Fe in 1803, condemning the *Contrato Social* by Juan Santiago Rousseau and another work called *La Borarquia o Víctima de la Inquisición*. The document warned that enemies of civil order were disseminating these depraved writings — containing liberty slogans and advocating independence — with the intention of destroying the Spanish "throne and altar." If the Governor found any such books in his jurisdiction, he was directed to send them to Chihuahua, placing them under lock and key so that no one could read them on the road south.[31]

These efforts by the Spanish Church and State to combat the spread of unorthodox literature in an out-of-the-way place like New Mexico appear more ludicrous than sinister. The simple frontier folk, concerned mainly with winning a living from the difficult soil and with preserving their lives in the face of constant Indian warfare, were hardly susceptible to subversion. They listened to the reading by the village priest or told tales around the campfire, and, for the time and place, that was all they required. For the most part, they were neither readers nor writers.

*Notes:*

1. George P. Hammond and Agapito Rey, eds. and trs., *Don Juan de Oñate, Colonizer of New Mexico, 1595–1628* (2 vols.; Albuquerque: University of New Mexico Press, 1953), I, 253.

2. *Ibid.,* I, 254; and Eleanor B. Adams and France V. Scholes, "Books in New Mexico, 1598–1680," *New Mexico Historical Review,* XVII (1942), p. 252.

3. Quoted in the Foreword by F. W. Hodge in Gaspar Pérez de Villagrá, *History of New Mexico* (trs. by Gilberto Espinosa; Los Angeles: The Quivira Society, 1933).

4. *Ibid.,* p. 267.

5. Ralph Emerson Twitchell, *Captain Don Gaspar de Villagrá* (Santa Fe: Historical Society of New Mexico, 1924), p. 10.

6. *Narratives of the Coronado Expedition, 1540–1542* (Albuquerque: University of New Mexico Press, 1940); *The Rediscovery of New Mexico, 1580–1594* (Albuquerque: University of New Mexico Press, 1966); and *Don Juan de Oñate,* cited above.

7. Henry R. Wagner, *The Spanish Southwest, 1542–1794* (2 vols.; Los Angeles: The Quivira Society, 1937), I, 232.

8. After publication of the Ayer edition, a revision of the *Memorial* in the handwriting of Benavides and dated February 12, 1634, was discovered in the Propaganda Archives in Rome. It has been translated and edited by Frederick Webb Hodge, George

P. Hammond, and Agapito Rey, as *Fray Alonso de Benavides' Revised Memorial of 1634* (Albuquerque: University of New Mexico Press, 1945). See also, F. W. Hodge, *Bibliography of Fray Alonso de Benavides* (New York: Museum of the American Indian, Heye Foundation, 1919).

9. Mrs. Edward E. Ayer, tr., *The Memorial of Fray Alonso de Benavides,* 1630 (Chicago: Privately Printed, 1916), pp. 22–23.

10. Eleanor B. Adams, "Two Colonial New Mexico Libraries, 1704, 1776." *New Mexico Historical Review,* XIX (1944), p. 151; and Paul Horgan, *Lamy of Santa Fe, His Life and Times* (New York: Farrar, Straus and Giroux, 1975), p. 414.

11. Lansing B. Bloom, "Fray Estevan de Perea's *Relacion,*" *New Mexico Historical Review,* VIII (1933), pp. 211–35.

12. Eleanor B. Adams and Fray Angelico Chavez, eds. and trs., *The Missions of New Mexico, 1776, a Description by Francisco Atanasio Domínguez* (Albuquerque: University of New Mexico Press, 1956), p. 256.

13. Quoted in Roland F. Dickey, "Paging Procrustes, an Adventure in the Making of a Book," *New Mexico Quarterly,* XXVI (1956), p. 59.

14. France V. Scholes, "Manuscripts for the History of New Mexico in the National Library in Mexico City," *New Mexico Historical Review,* III (1928), p. 321.

15. "Paging Procrustes," p. 69.

16. Adams, "Two Colonial New Mexico Libraries," p. 146; and Adams and Chavez, *Missions of New Mexico,* pp. 220ff.

17. Robert Ricard, *The Spiritual Conquest of Mexico* (Berkeley and Los Angeles: University of California Press, 1966), p. 50.

18. See Gerónimo Zárate Salmerón, *Relaciones* (tr. by Alicia Ronstadt Milich; Albuquerque: Horn and Wallace, 1966). This work is a summary history of New Mexico down to the year 1626.

19. H. Bailey Carroll and J. Villasana Haggard, trs. and eds., *Three New Mexico Chronicles* (Albuquerque: The Kuivira Society, 1942). This book contains a facsimile of Pino's work, pp. 211–61, in addition to the translation.

20. France V. Scholes, "Church and State in New Mexico," *New Mexico Historical Review,* XI (1936), p. 316.

21. Adams and Scholes, "Books in New Mexico," pp. 231–32.

22. France V. Scholes, *Troublous Times in New Mexico, 16591670* (Albuquerque: University of New Mexico Press, 1942). The Inquisition's court recorder seems to have made a slip by attributing *Orlando Furioso* to Tasso. Torquato Tasso was author of another popular Italian work, *Jerusalem Liberated.*

23. Adams and Scholes, "Books in New Mexico," p. 244.

24. Scholes, *Troublous Times,* p. 162.

25. *Ibid.,* p. 168.

26. Adams and Scholes, "Books in New Mexico," p. 251.

27. Sigüenza y Góngora also wrote a journalistic account of the successful reconquest of New Mexico in 1692. Irving Albert Leonard, ed. and tr., *The Mercurio Volante of Don Carlos de Sigüenza y Góngora* (Los Angeles: The Quivira Society, 1932).

28. Irving A. Leonard, *Baroque Times in Old Mexico* (Ann Arbor: University of Michigan Press, 1966), p. 88.

29. Adams and Scholes, "Books in New Mexico," pp. 229–30.

30. Copy of a Royal Decree, Chihuahua, Nov. 4, 1778, Spanish Archives of New Mexico, doc. no. 749; State Records Center and Archives, Santa Fe.

31. Nemesio Salcedo to the Governor of New Mexico, Chihuahua, Nov. 1, 1803, Spanish Archives of New Mexico, doc. no. 1686; State Records Center and Archives, Santa Fe.

# VOICES FROM THE SOUTHWEST

Sarah Bouquet

✤ 🙰 ✤

WOMEN TODAY ARE KEENLY INTERESTED IN THEMSELVES. This interest might be self-consciousness only, or it might be evidence of a wider and deeper preoccupation. Our society is boiling in ferment and confused by rapid change. If any one of us is a responsible person, he or she must consider every action every day as a contribution toward the future. We are all going through the Looking Glass and my thesis is that women, far more than men, are concerned with the rationale behind the things they do, the choices they make in daily living. The current women's movement is nothing more than a serious rethinking of people's lives and habits since our culture has been changing so unpredictably and rapidly.

Women feel like pioneers today. Fortunately they are not in uncharted territory. The people of the Southwest, still so varied and unstructured a group, are the inheritors of a recent pioneer tradition: the savagery of this frontier is a part of modern consciousness. The land of the Southwest still calls for accommodation and respect; it has not been tamed. A way of life must still be designed to suit the land and can still be designed to suit the individual. For this reason, those who have recently lived the same adventure can speak to us with great meaning. Women's accounts of making a new life in the arid lands can show us what they found to be most important. Even a vacation offers a new view of oneself and of one's way of life, but a total relocation can melt one in a crucible.

The question is, can we learn anything about what has remained important through history? We aren't unique or alone; we can compare ourselves with our ancestors in varieties of ways. Distant women can tell us about the essence of their experiences and we can find our common bonds comforting and perhaps informative. There are many voices, many ways of self-presentation: the intimacy of the journal or family letter, the personal or very abstract history, or the intuition of the fiction writer. Only the last has been ruled out as a source of information. In actual accounts of traveling and settling we can hear voices speaking to us and test them against our own perceptions. What do they say to us?

They say they tried to do their best for their children. They looked to the future. This absorption gave seriousness to their lives. Until recently women had no choices about having children and no guidance, other than traditional religion and rigid social norms: both of which were absent on the early frontiers. These women had to devise, invent and hope for the best. They had to decide how much of their past to retain for ballast and how much to give up for a new life. There are many expressions of strong family feeling and commitment. Here are excerpts from a sad set of private letters which were written by a woman homesteading on the Plains, not all the way to the Southwest, but her comments are poignant and yet show the purpose that helped people adapt. These letters were written in 1857:

> Mother has been homesick ever since we left Whitins. She thinks of all places the West is *Most Miserable*. I am sorry she ever came here, for I don't think she ever will like. Today and yesterday she has been down to the lowest notch. . . . She says tell you never to think of leaving old Conn. for the sake of coming out West where there is nothing but land. And she thinks it rather hard to sacrifice everything for a little land.
>
> It is one year today since we left our New England home to find a home in this Western World. I have had a great many sad hours and shed many tears. It never has seemed like home to me yet, but hope it will be better for my family.[1]

Of all the things these passages reveal, the strongest is Betsy Rist's sense of the flow of time toward the future; her sense of sacrifice for eventual better life.

Many reminiscences are concerned with food, shelter, modes of travel, and self-protection. People were forced to subsist on very little and to risk their lives continually. Simple exposure could exaggerate any other physical problem and Indians were a constant threat for many years. Over and over, however, there is evidence of women not only enduring and providing for their children's daily welfare, but of actual relish in the challenge.

Of course, those who survived and who kept their family histories were probably the most vigorous and inventive, not to mention the luckiest.

Food is the great common element in the accounts from the nineteenth-century Southwest. Martha Summerhayes, Mrs. Granville Oury, Mrs. Biddle, and others refer constantly to the challenge of providing a nutritious and varied diet without cooling, without choices, and without equipment. Almost all the reminiscences I read, even including those from more recent years, contained recipes and descriptions of methods of preserving and cooling, even those of the wealthy Mabel Luhan of Taos, New Mexico. The most ingenious suggestions were Mrs. Biddle's recipes for custard without eggs or milk and apple pie made without apples. "You will feel sure it is apple-pie (if you do not make it yourself)."[2] And further, any woman who could cook seemed to have felt obligated to provide for any person in the vicinity. Ma'am Jones of New Mexico is the greatest example of generous feeding. Men were also fine cooks, especially camp cooks, but little concerned with variety and invention; they were just supporting life, not enriching it. The time and effort given by so many women is a moving thought. Feeding the human animal is a simple matter, but the serious application of the mind to cooking can be seen as an act of love.

There is, by contrast, a strange ambivalence to be seen in the dangers to which families exposed their children. The Southwest was the setting for the most protracted Indian wars, and Indians were an increasing threat for decades. Only a very overwhelming need to push on and settle could have driven people through some of the events they describe. What did the mother of Owen P. White feel as she checked the cyanide pills in her locket before going through a particularly dangerous pass on the way to Tucson?[3] She was willing to kill herself and her children to prevent giving that pleasure to the Apaches — all in order to get to a new home. Other women, Mrs. Oury, Martha Summerhayes, and many others describe well the fright of riding through territory known to be extremely dangerous. Frequently a woman would say, later, she didn't know how or why they were lucky: they had honestly expected to die. What a risk for an unknown future; did the past drive them or the future draw them?

Loneliness was a more insidious enemy than danger. Mrs. Granville Oury was in a wagon for weeks as she moved through Mexico toward Tucson after the Civil War: "Again I am at a loss for employment. O! for something to read. In sheer desperation I must make somebody else some shirts. . . . Goodness! what am I to do with myself, the sun is pouring down without mercy or remorse and I am being roasted alive. Not a tree within ten miles. Not a breath of air stirring. The ambulance is standing on a sheet

35

of white ground. God deliver me from another sight of this portion of Mexico."[4] She is a sensible yet sensitive woman, and frequently had a hard time making good use of herself in a continually changing environment. Susan Magoffin, a lone woman with her Army husband, on the first U.S. penetration to Santa Fe in the 1840s, expresses another kind of frustration: "Wrote a long letter to Mama this evening. I do wish I could have a letter from home; how lonely it is, week after week and month after month, and I hear nothing, more than if I never belonged to their numbers. 'twould indeed give new energy to my being to hear from them, quite a new creature I should feel but as it is I am perfectly isolated."[5] These needs to be useful and for family comforts go deep and reflect the hardest kind of disorientation. In the early twentieth century Hilda France was moving south into Navajo land to start a trading post with her husband and observed the women whose wagons they passed: "A lump comes into my throat when I remember the loneliness and hardship, fortitude and courage of those settlers of Utah. I shut my eyes and see the faces of the women we met. They were tired always, but determined, and had a look that made me think they were more isolated by something inside them than by geographical conditions."[6] All these women speak directly to us over the many years.

But these deprivations were a great equalizer. When people did have a chance to get together, they shared everything. The same Susan Magoffin describes meeting another woman, very shortly after her expression of loneliness in her journal: they talk and talk, take off their clothes, lie down together for their siesta and keep right on talking.[7] Another face of this feeling is the neighborliness which is sentimentally remembered and described repeatedly. People took care of each other; Ma'am Jones rode off with her tiny baby to nurse an entire family devastated by smallpox.[8] Another woman, reports Sharlot Hall, gave her white satin wedding gown and the fine wood box of a music box to make a casket for a baby, giving up cherished things she'd hauled across the country to comfort a stranger.[9]

It is a short step, from loneliness to neighborliness, to the beginnings of communities. How did the lonely, land-seeking settlers recombine with others and become townspeople? Women are generally credited with the organizing impulse; "hardly would two women come together without planning schools, church schools, entertainment, lending books and helping in sickness and death."[10] It was women who pressed for better sanitation, regulations for cleanliness in food stores, and other improvements, and it took a while to break the casual habits of the frontier: "it was not all at once that we have reached our present standard of civic housekeeping."[11] All kinds of women concerned themselves with their communities: "but however crude the life women lived, they brought amenities. . . . The 'Chippies' at Hillsboro subscribed most of the money that opened the first church in Kingston."[12] Schools and churches had a purpose; they were necessary to the better life and to the sense of the future.

Once "amenities" and a peaceful community were established, however, the inevitable social separations took place. Again, women were thinking ahead and designing environments for their children. Young children were taught not to look under saloon doors and to feel horrified by the existence of prostitutes. Irene Cornwall Cofer describes a girlhood encounter in New Mexico with the town madam in a classic combination of childish honesty with learned moral judgment:

> One day I met one of these "women" on a narrow trail, a small dog was trotting along behind her. Intuition told me who she was as I knew everyone else in town. I went in to my act as "nice little girls" should, head just at the angle to see all you could and not appear inquisitive, when a soft voice said "Goodmorning, Baby" (I was eight years old). I stopped and looked with both eyes; no horns, just a neatly dressed middle aged woman wearing hat and gloves. A thought ran through my childish mind, maybe this is "Blackjack."
>
> I have wondered since if this refined looking woman, who could have been anyone's mother, had not at one time been respected and known a better life.[13]

The mix of humanity which had existed on the raw frontier quickly separated into oil and water as life grew more complex. But the emulsion had its effect and is still held in fond memory.

A most dramatic and recent example of community feeling growing after the lonely Western life is the life of Edith Warner. She came to New Mexico in the 1930s to find health and found her own spiritual and personal home. The outgrowth of that, however, was the development of her maternal feelings, not only for her Indian companion, Tilano, her friends at the San Ildefonso Pueblo, but also for the scientists of Los Alamos for whom she provided an oasis during World War II. Her preoccupation with food, her famous chocolate cake, for example, is an extension of this feeling; indeed she was quite a creative maker of her home; "yet each year I do less and less of the customary things of our civilization."[14] Her experience is almost a paradigm of the renaissance that can come about when a person has been stripped down by experience and has then rebuilt by slow states of experiment and affirmation.

Not everyone can respond to the challenge to reform their patterns, to seek the "magic of an environment created by ourselves,"[15] as Mabel Dodge Luhan expresses it. A daughter describes a mother who came west to Tucson and who never changed; "Poor Mother! I can see her today in her riding habit with full black bloomers, black stockings, and hat primly tied down with a veil — just moseying along and looking most uncomfortable. Mother remained a New Englander. She lived in Arizona more than forty years but never did become westernized."[16] A contemporary Tucson woman can honestly say, "I never liked it out here; not a day has passed that I haven't missed my home in Michigan." Perhaps some were happier before they moved; perhaps other were inflexible, but many women found great joy in surmounting the challenges. Many look back with nostalgia on the hard times; as a woman remarked about her life in New Mexico before the turn of the century, "A friend once remarked that it was surprising how comfortable we were with nothing on earth to make us comfortable."[17]

Some people are adaptable, then, but the next question is, what were they, and are they, doing in the Southwest? What forces brought them here and, finally, once here, what other forces are there peculiar to this region?

As to what brought people here originally, the strongest single force for women in the nineteenth century was their concept of marriage. Whether their husbands were Army men, farmers, ranchers, or miners, throughout the nineteenth century, women were here because their husbands were. The most dramatic evidence for this is not in their statements of whither thou goest I will go, which are easy to find, but in their utter identification with their husbands. They do not record their own stories. Mattie Lloyd Wooten's *Women Tell the Story of the Southwest* is a long series of short pieces by women, and almost all are stories of the bravery and fortitude of men. The saga of life in the West was a man's epic struggle; their families were unquestioning and adoring.

The men wanted land.

> Like many young couples who lived in stock raising countries which were constantly becoming overcrowded, we decided the only remedy to solve our problems was to do as many others had been forced to do. . . . "Go West."[18]

The land beckoned, the grass was deep, and the Indians hadn't cut into it; they had lived with it but had not possessed it. Any search through nineteenth century attitudes toward the land reveals the sexuality of the settler's desires. Lily Klasner's father saw a beautiful valley in New Mexico and "decided that he would take that land."[19] The Civil War was a real catalyst, but the rape of the American West was already fated: fresh land, pure

38

springs and limitless potential were too alluring. And women felt it too —
they share responsibility for this grasping. Mrs. Biddle's comments as an
Army wife seem a little repellent:

> The army has not been given the credit it deserves, but the world is
> now fast awakening to the realisation that the Regular Army has been
> the great factor in building up, and for the progress in general of the
> great West. Soldiers made it possible for the great railways to be built
> across the Continent; they guarded the workmen from Indians, while
> they laid the rails and afterwards, so that the rails should not be torn up,
> sleeping on bare ground with only their blankets wrapped around them,
> often suffering from cold and exposure. The isolated army post made it
> practicable for the pioneer and early settler to take up ground, raise cattle
> and till the soil, for he, too, was protected by the soldier.[20]

Later the mines brought men and women too, but once towns had been
formed almost any reason could draw people to the area. Though there had
been single women and widow homesteaders, in the twentieth century
more women came to the Southwest alone. Georgia O'Keefe is a good
example. After World War II, Alice Marriott wrote about her arrival.

> Maybe, I mused, we are part of a postwar back-to-the-soil movement.
> Maybe we are in our miniscule selves an expression of a larger dissatis-
> faction with urban life that many people seem to feel at this time. Per-
> haps we incorporate in our persons one phase of the destruction the city
> wreaks upon itself when it drives out the souls that find creation impos-
> sible in urban surroundings.[21]

At the same time, women who are linked as firmly to their husbands as
were the settlers' wives are growing more self-aware. Mary Rak, an Arizona ranchwoman, is a good example. Their basic concerns are still with
order and purpose. Eulalia Bourne, an Arizona contemporary, writes about
her teaching, "with no children of my own and a driving passion for improving human beings."[22] Whatever their occupation, women have become
more reflective in more recent times, more interested in themselves. The
basic response to the challenge to find new ways of life is the same, however.

Having considered some of the factors which motivate women and a few
of the historical forces which have had influence, we must turn to a consideration of the Southwest itself as a participant in this passage of time and in
women's lives. It was at its most vivid and alien when the first few white
women saw it; women such as Susan Magoffin and Martha Summerhayes,

traveling with the military spearhead of the coming invasion. What did they find and think about?

Unlike any other section of the West, the Southwest has two well-established native populations, several tribes of Indians and Mexican settlers. Since the Southwest was settled slowly and sparsely, newcomers were forced to accommodate themselves to those who already were settled and who had strong cultural patterns of their own. It is doubtful whether any other section of our country had similar sedentary occupants and a few towns already established when the first white settlers arrived.

Mrs. Granville Oury and Martha Summerhayes are examples of the extremes of response to the natives of the Southwest. Mrs. Oury describes her reactions to Mexicans and Indians in priggish, ethnocentric terms: as a Southern Belle. Seeing naked Mexican men diving and swimming to help ferry loads across a river "excited my disgust."[23] And Indians are even more unpleasant: "All my ideas of them were borrowed from Cooper's novels, I watched their movements with curious interest, which very soon resolved itself into extreme disgust and abhorrence. Ugh! the filthy horrid creatures, and the most persistent 'beggars' I ever saw. . . . I spent a sleepless night, haunted by the sight of those horrid, loathsome creatures."[24]

Finally, her reaction to post-Civil War Tucson reveals her limitations perfectly: "I look around me with a sinking heart and wonder if this can be the goal we have been striving so hard to reach. Excepting the wretched, squalid town of Janos in Mex, . . . I do not remember of ever having seen a less inviting, less promising prospect for a home. Tucson is certainly the most forsaken spot of earth ever trodden by the foot of a white man."[25] She needs not to be surprised by life; she needs predictability.

Martha Summerhayes is a very different woman. She has not only the curiosity of an open mind, she had the flexibility of a creative one. Her thoughts on Mexican women's clothes are a fine example: "I often cried: 'Oh! if I could only dress as the Mexicans do! Their necks and arms do look so cool and clean.'

"I have always been sorry I did not adopt their fashion of house apparel. Instead of that, I yielded to the prejudices of my conservative partner, and sweltered during the day in high-necked and long-sleeved white dresses."[26] And her pride in acceptance of her servant Charley are symbolic of a mind that transcends the unexpected and loves all the ways of the world:

[Friends] were always astonished when the Cocopah Indian waited on them at the table, for he wore nothing but his geestring, and although it was an everyday matter to us, it rather took their breath away.

But "Charley" appealed to my aesthetic sense in every way. Tall, and well-made, with clean-cut limbs and features, fine smooth copper-colored skin, handsome face, heavy black hair done up in pompadour fashion and plastered with Colorado mud, which was baked white by the sun. . . ."[27]

Almost more than any other woman she could appreciate otherness, without romanticizing and without selfconsciously inflated language.

Few settlers had any feeling for Indians at all, but many comment on the politeness of the Mexican people. Anglo men married Mexican women during the late nineteenth century; one guess suggests as many as ninety percent married Mexican women in New Mexico.[28] Dorothy Pillsbury expresses a sympathy and preference for Mexican workmen in her adobe home, "native workmen accept the whimsicalities of little adobe houses with respect, understanding, and a reciprocal gaiety."[29]

Mary Austin has an optimistic view of the cultural blend:

Three strains of comparative purity lie here in absorbing contact . . . for by distance, by terror of vastness and raw surfaces, the more timorous, least adaptive elements of our population are strained out.[30]

And many women, as Edith Warner did, have felt a deep, intuitive kinship with the Navajo or Pueblo Indians. A few of the most "adaptive," such as Mabel Dodge Luhan, have married Indian men, but this is largely a twentieth-century development.

The next characteristic of the Southwest is that while life here requires flexibility and some stamina, it offers good health. From the earliest commentator to the most recent, women have rejoiced in the air and the cleanliness of the simple life. Susan Magoffin gives the air some moral powers: "Oh, this is a life I would not exchange for a good deal! There is such independence, so much free and uncontaminated air, which impregnates the mind, the feelings, nay every thought, with purity. I breathe free without that oppression and uneasiness felt in the gossiping circles of a settled home."[31]

A similar thought, and more joyous prose, "Oh, sugar, is wasn't nothing, driving that team. . . . It was a sight easier than washing clothes on a fire in the yard, back home in Kansas. It was fun. And clean! My lands, you never saw a country so clean. Until you've walked on land that's never been broken, and smelled air that's never been breathed, you don't know what clean is".[32]

Mrs. Biddle comments on her daughter's health in a voice one might not expect from a Victorian Lady who fainted regularly, "She was quite tall for her age, rode well, and was perfectly fearless, also hearty and strong, owing to the outdoor life in that wonderful climate."[33] Alice Marriott's is a darker and more contemporary comment on why she would stay in New Mexico, "The working conditions we had found were good for us both. As our physical health improved with the simple life we led, we found that we could face new days and the problems that they brought us without wanting to run away from both."[34]

And, finally, there is the land itself. Unseasonal and uncomfortable, the plants have a force all their own. Mrs. Oury noticed a presence in the Sonoran cacti, "But the terror of both man and beast in Mexico is the thorns. Everything is armed with them. The sharpest, longest, fiercest thorns in the world. You can't avoid them, they are everywhere, on everything. The very atmosphere seems to bristle with them."[35]

Mary Austin feels them even more acutely, "As if all their secret processes were primed to catch the advantage of the rainy hour, the desert growth produces in the observer a sense of desertness. This curious feeling of aliveness of the plant world, waiting like a cat creature of the cat kind, every shrub and tree clawed like a cat, crouched for the spring. . . ."[36] But more astonishing still are the mountains; there is no human quality there, though imagery of the body comes easily, "I know that no wooded, verdant country could make me feel as this one does. Its very nudity makes it intimate. . . . I think I could not bear again great masses of growing things . . . it would stifle me as buildings do."[37]

Peggy Pond Church, in a personal letter to L. C. Powell, carries Edith Warner's image of nudity even further, "Perhaps what we most appreciate in our arid landscape is the essential bony structure of the country, all that rocky geometry, those planes and angles that do such beautiful things with the light. What has always impressed me is the feeling of vast movements of time."[38]

What do all these women's voices tell us about ourselves? That we are a complex blend. We are open to new places and people and patterns but carry much useful and useless baggage from the past. That we are ingenious both in our flexibility and in our rigidity. We are designed to survive, perhaps even to flourish, blessed to be able to do so in this setting.

There is something diminishing to us in this open landscape; we are vulnerable and our time is short. Yet there is also liberation in the openness and acrid dryness. One feels one's self expand when the body is so belittled. Some people must resent this; they find Eastern style homes, lawn sprinkler systems and people of their own, old ilk a bulwark against strangeness. But the true pioneers and dwellers in the desert are those whose hearts and minds are open to everyone and larger than everything. Owen P. White said of his mother, "My intense admiration for my mother was not because she could do everything, but because she understood everything. Her life on the frontier had made her as big, and broad, and capable as a strong man without taking away from her any of the attributes of a true woman."[39]

It is marvelous to see such depths and breadths in women and to hope that we too will be able to "understand everything," thorns and all. The Southwest bristles and bakes and echoes with itself. The land reminds us that our tragedies are acted on a tiny stage. It's a comforting thought. Perhaps we grasp here, after the general rape of the West, something which wouldn't be had, something which remains and will remain itself, indifferent, transcendent, and eternal.

*Notes:*

1. Unpublished letters of Betsy Rist, 1857.

2. Ellen McGowan Biddle, *Reminiscences of a Soldier's Wife*, J. B. Lippencott Co., Philadelphia, 1907, p. 173.

3. Owen P. White, *A Frontier Mother*, Minton, Balch and Co,. New York, 1929, p. 68.

4. Mrs. Granville Oury, "Some Unpublished History of the Southwest," *Arizona Historical Review*, Jan. 1932, p. 54.

5. Susan Shelby Magoffin, *Down the Santa Fe Trail and Into Mexico*, Yale University Press, New Haven, 1926, p. 236.

6. Hilda Faunce, *Desert Wife*, Little, Brown, and Co., Boston, 1934, p. 34.

7. Magoffin, *op. cit.*, p. 251.

8. Eve Ball, *Ma'am Jones of the Pecos*, University of Arizona Press, Tucson, Ariz., 1969, p. 45.

9. Mattie Lloyd Wooten, *Women Tell the Story of the Southwest*, The Naylor Co., San Antonio, Texas, 1940, p. 334.

10. *Ibid.*, p. 333.

11. James D. Shinkle, *Reminiscences of Roswell Pioneers*, Hall-Poorbaugh Press, Roswell, New Mexico, 1966, p. 181.

12. Erna Fergusson, *New Mexico*, Alfred A. Knopf, New York, 1951, p. 292.

13. Irene Cornwall Cofer, *The Lunch Tree*, Theo. Gaus & Sons, New York, 1969, pp. 20–21.

14. Peggy Pond Church, *The House at Otowi Bridge*, University of New Mexico Press, Albuquerque, N.M., 1960, p. 41.

15. Mabel Dodge Luhan, *Winter in Taos*, Sage Books, Inc., Denver, 1935, p. 157.

16. E. O. Stratton and Edith Stratton Kitt, *Pioneering in Arizona*, Arizona Pioneers Historical Society, Tucson, Ariz., 1964, p. 134.

17. Shinkle, *op. cit.,* p. 177.

18. *Ibid.,* p. 104.

19. Lily Klasner, *My Girlhood Among Outlaws,* University of Arizona Press, Tucson, Ariz., 1972, p. 76.

20. Biddle, *op. cit.,* p. 208.

21. Alice Marriott, *The Valley Below,* University of Oklahoma Press, Norman, Okla., 1949, p. 11.

22. Eulalia Bourne, *Kids and Cows,* Arizona Cattlelog, Oct., 1951, p. 6.

23. Oury, *op. cit.,* p. 59.

24. *Ibid.,* p. 63.

25. *Ibid.,* p. 61.

26. Martha Summerhayes, *Vanished Arizona,* The Rio Grande Press, Glorieta, N.M., 1970, p. 158.

27. *Ibid.,* p. 162.

28. Shinkle, *op. cit.,* p. 92.

29. Dorothy L. Pillsbury, *Roots in Adobe,* University of New Mexico Press, Albuquerque, N.M., 1959, p. 106.

30. Mary Austin, *Land of Journey's Ending,* The Century Co., New York, 1924, p. 442.

31. Magoffin, *op. cit.,* p. 10.

32. Robert West Howard, ed., *This is the West,* Signet Book, published by New American Library, N.Y., 1957, p. 99.

33. Biddle, *op. cit.,* p. 188.

34. Marriott, *op. cit.,* p. 61.

35. Oury, *op. cit.,* p. 51.

36. Austin, *op. cit.,* pp. 156–57.

37. Church, *op. cit.,* p. 13.

38. Peggy Pond Church, unpublished letter to LCP, 1974.

39. White, *op. cit.,* p. 101.

# THE FACES AND FORCES
# OF PIMERIA ALTA

Bernard L. Fontana

❖⳹❖

Part of the northernmost reaches of the Sonoran Desert takes its single name from the human inhabitants whose home was here at the opening of the historic period in the late seventeenth century. Spaniards called them "Sobaipuris," "Sobas," "Ymuris," "Piatos," "Gileños," "Papagos," and "Pimas." These labels tended to shield the underlying cultural and social realities as practiced and perceived by the natives themselves. Their universal concept of self was encapsulated in the single term, *o-odham,* which means, quite simply, "people." But there were many different groups of *o-odham,* and by no means were the groups necessarily as Europeans named them to be.

These people, Pimans, as they have come to be known, had linguistic and cultural relatives far to the south in what are today the Mexican states of Sonora, Chihuahua, Sinaloa, Nayarit, and Durango. A few *o-odham* were called Tepecanos; more were thought of as Tepehuanes. Still others were natives whom Spaniards called Pimas. When additional people were found far to the north who spoke dialects of the same language, some of the southerners became the Pimas Bajos and the northerns the Pimas Altos. Their respective lands, in turn, came to be Pimería Baja and Pimería Alta. Thus the northern Sonoran Desert is Pimería Alta, the land of the Upper Piman Indians.

How new were the faces of Piman Indians in the Sonoran Desert in the seventeenth century? There are almost as many theories on the subject of

Piman prehistory as there are theorizers. The honest answer, however, continues to be that we simply do not know. What is sure is that when they were first seen by literate Europeans their various lifestyles were quite unlike that manifested by river-dwelling Hohokam, those city-dwelling makers of fine pottery — and creators of exceptional art in other forms as well — who subjugated vast acres of desert terrain with their monumental irrigation works. To the extent that their lifestyles differed from that of two or three centuries earlier, then, the Pimans were "new" to the northern Sonoran Desert in the sixteenth or seventeenth centuries.

What were they like, these people whom we think of today as desert dwellers par excellence?

First of all, there were three major different groups of Upper Pimans as defined by differing adaptations to three major sub-environments within the region. These sub-environments are those characterized by the presence of perennial streams; those where there are seasonally reliable ephemeral streams and from five to ten inches of annual rainfall; and a large area where annual rainfall is from zero to five inches and where ephemeral stream flow is so small and erratic that farming or gardening with the use of surface water is an impossibility.

The latter area lies entirely within the Lower Colorado Valley vegetation zone of the Sonoran Desert. Its hallmarks are the creosote bush and white bursage, giving it the label of "little-leaved" desert. The part of it being considered here is bounded roughly by the lower Gila River on the north, the Gila Mountains on the west, the Growler Mountains on the east, and the head of the Gulf of California on the south.

The Pimans native to this driest of desert regions, known to us in more recent times as the Sand Papagos, were hunting-gathering-trading nomads. They had no fixed habitations but rather lived in seasonal camps never too far from the few natural springs in the area or from natural granite water catchment basins called *tinajas*. In season they were at the head of the Gulf of California living on shellfish, gathering salt and shells for trade, and spearing fish stranded in tide pools. At other times they were inland, gathering roots, seeds, edible leaves and other vegetable foods, and hunting and trapping small game, including lizards. Their trade was with Yuman Indians, agricultural peoples living on the Lower Colorado River. To get Yuman pottery and farm products they gave salt, shells, and ceremonial songs and dances.

Although we have no population estimates for Sand Papagos by their European contemporaries, there were probably never more than 500 of them. Population density would necessarily have been extremely low. They were possibly divided into bands comprised of extended families; membership in particular camps was probably flexible. In 1701 a party of Spaniards found a band of some fifty people living in the Pincate Mountains in northwestern Sonora who were said to be "poor and naked [and] who sustain themselves by roots, locusts and lizards, and some fish." Fifty may have been close to the optimum band size.

The Sand Papagos, the last of the Great North American Desert's truly nomadic people, lapsed into history in the early part of the twentieth century. Many died from yellow fever in 1851; others were killed by travelers through their country; and still others wandered off to lose themselves among the populations of both Indian and non-Indian settlements along their borders.

The remainder of Pimería Alta falls within the Arizona Upland vegetation zone of the Sonoran Desert except for a few segments on the east, such as the San Pedro Valley, which is generally beyond the desert. Although the creosote bush continues to dominate in the plains and lower foothills, this zone is characterized by such plants as the saguaro; a wide range of Opuntias, including the chollas and prickly pears; and by trees such as mesquites, ironwood, and palo verdes. It is a "stem-succulent" desert.

While the vegetation has generally uniform characteristics, the Arizona Upland region has two major sub-environments: that of perennial and intermittent streams and that with only ephemeral streams. The latter is the heartland of those Pimans we known as Papago Indians. They were a two-village people who lived near permanent springs in the mountains and foothills during the winter and who lived in farming settlements next to their agricultural fields in the inter-montane valleys during the summer rainy season. To grow their crops they planted at the mouths of arroyos where the onrushing water would spread over their fields. If needed, they would build temporary brush dams better to control the water. These were arroyo-mouth or *ak chin* farmers, and their method of raising crops is called *ak chin* agriculture. Their field was an *oidak* or, in Spanish, a *temporal*. Mountain ranges served as great collectors of summer's torrential rains; the arroyos were the pipes and canals to conduct the water, often for as many as ten to fifteen miles; gravity was the pump. Papago crops were maize, beans, and cucurbits.

When the harvest was over and the summer rain ponds were dry, the people either returned to their winter villages or wandered afar to visit or trade with neighboring peoples. They supplemented their farm produce with the fruits of hunting and gathering. Or, more properly, they supplemented their hunting and gathering with the foods they could grow.

47

With the river-dwelling peoples whom the Spaniards called Pimas and Sobaipuris, the situation was not unlike that for the desert Papagos except that two-village people became essentially one-village people. Their rivers assured them a permanent source of drinking water even if their summer crops did not afford them a means to farm in all seasons. Some of these Pimans may have been irrigation farmers before the advent of European influence, but we cannot be sure. It is just as possible that they were essentially floodplain farmers, relying on the widening of rivers in flood season to water their fields rather than on any very elaborate system of ditching.

Villages, and these were the largest settlements recorded for aboriginal Pimans, tended to be fixed and permanent, located at places on the rivers where the water always surfaced along an otherwise sometimes intermittent course of surface flow. If a crop should fail, being washed away, a village might have become wholly or partially abandoned while its residents intensified their hunting or gathering or moved in among more fortunate neighbors. Even in good years, Pimans continued to hunt and to collect wild plant foods as if their lives depended on it, as, indeed, they did. Their agriculture seems not to have been intensive enough to sustain them throughout the year.

It has been estimated that at the end of the seventeenth century and the beginning of the eighteenth century, in two specific areas adjacent to the middle Gila River between its junction with the Salt River and Casa Grande ruins, there were at most a thousand Pima Indians who lived here in three villages. It has been further estimated that eighteen bushels of maize would be required to support one adult for a year, and that early Piman maize yielded only about ten to twelve bushels per acre per year. This means that about 1,800 acres would have had to have been planted in maize to support a thousand people. Considering the areas involved, 1,800 acres is only a fraction — less than a third in the most generous estimate — of the land which would have been available for floodwater agriculture, that is, land which would not have had to have been irrigated to get a successful crop.

The point of this is that the resources of the northern Sonoran Desert were sufficient to support the native peoples who lived in it provided they were willing — as Pimans clearly were — to adjust their population densities, settlement patterns, and food-getting and distribution strategies in such a way as to take sub-environmental conditions into account.

Moreover, Pimans practiced what anthropologist Ruth Underhill referred to as an economy of abundance. Food resources were shared reciprocally not only by members of immediate families, but by members of extended families, of villages, and of inter-related villages as well. Pimans were obliged to give as well as to receive. Sharing with members of one's own family was obligatory and unquestioned. Generosity meant an investment in one's fellow human beings. Stinginess, an investment in material wealth, meant isolation and possible death. The desert demands cooperation of its human dwellers.

Sharing with members of other communities took the form of gift exchanges and of inter-village games and contests in which participants and onlookers bet on the outcome. The people were great gamblers, winning and losing often enough to assure an equitable distribution of resources over a large number of the members of the society.

Pimans were possessed of durable goods, those living on the rivers owning more artifacts than the two-village people, and far more than the hunter-gatherer nomads of the west. Wasting and hoarding, however, meaning the accumulation of surplus wealth, were frowned upon and there were societal sanctions against them. Water, the most precious resource in the desert, was husbanded carefully and treated with utmost ceremonial and factual respect. All the architecture, for example, was dry. Houses of brush, grass, and parts of trees were more than sufficient for shelter and privacy. Pimans felt no need to build structures of mud, even on rivers where water was available. Moreover, virtually all ceremonies other than those for curing had as their ultimate goal the bringing down of rain. Expeditions to the Gulf of California, ostensibly to gather salt from seashore deposits which lie there, have been immortalized in Papago song:

> By the sandy water I breathe in the odor of the sea,
> From there the wind comes and blows over the world,
> By the sandy water I breathe in the odor of the sea,
> From there the clouds come and rain falls over the world.

In sum, these Pimans of the northern Sonoran Desert applied the force of their knowledge of the desert surround as well as mobility, a low population density, and an ethic of sharing and interpersonal relationships to fashion for themselves ways of living which they perceived as satisfactory and meaningful. Furthermore, they accomplished this with materials at hand in the desert: their food, clothing, and shelter were products of the desert. Their economies were self-contained; their corporations were closed.

But this was not to last. At the end of the seventeenth century there came new faces and new forces to the Sonoran Desert, those representing the Crown of Spain in the form of missionaries, soldiers, and, in time, Spanish settlers. The vanguard of this newness in Pimería Alta was a Jesuit priest named Eusebio Kino. He came in 1687.

Among the many items that Kino and his colonial successors brought with them to the desert were new levers to use in an attempt to pry a surplus as well as a subsistence from the arid surroundings. Indeed, in large part they misread the true character of the Sonoran Desert with its erratic fluctuations in climate and its wildly varying micro-environments. They brought with them the products of an old and different world: chick peas, lentils, cowpeas, bastard chick peas, cabbages, lettuce, onions, leeks, garlic, anise, pepper, mustard, mint, sugar cane, grapevines, roses, and lilies. And what would life in a mission settlement have been without its figs, pomegranates, apricots, plums, quinces, pecans, peaches, pears, and apples? To say nothing of chocolate, especially for the Swiss Jesuits in the service of Spain?

So, too, came horses, oxen, pigs, mules, burros, chickens, domestic sheep and goats and cattle to Pimería Alta. The horses, mules, and burros would provide new means of transportation and beasts of burden. Oxen could pull the Spanish-introduced plow. The cattle, chickens, sheep, and goats could become the food gathers, converting the energy of wild plants into more ready-made and concentrated energy in the form of meat for human consumption.

Above all, perhaps, the Spaniards introduced wheat and barley. Wheat, unlike maize, could be raised as a winter crop. It was more easily grown than maize and its yields for the same expenditure of human effort were greater. And with new Spanish crops, most notably wheat, came what to the Pimas were probably new methods of farming. They began to dig ditches and to install extensive irrigation networks where there had been none before. More lands were put under cultivation. New forms of social and political organization had to be devised to cope with the new technology. Someone had to make decisions about where water should be put into certain fields and when. Labor forces had to be mobilized in ways that were novel.

Spanish efforts were so successful in implementing a whole new agriculture in Pimería Alta that within a month after Kino's arrival in 1687 the Pima Indians in the village of Remedios said they didn't want a priest because they would be required to spend too much time in sowing crops. Moreover, they asserted, so many cattle were being pastured that the waterholes were drying up. The Pimas, who had witnessed the effects of new crops and cattle among the Opata Indians south of them on the Río San Miguel, recognized mixed blessings when they saw them.

By the mid-eighteenth century the Gila River Pimas, even though no mission nor any kind of Spanish settlement had been founded among them, were busy raising Spanish wheat in addition to native maize. In wheat they sensed a force which helped them to level out normal desert fluctuations in production. They broadened their economic base to such an extent that by 1858, at which time their villages had become part of the United States, they were able to sell 100,000 pounds of wheat to troops and others in southern Arizona. The next year they sold 250,000 pounds. In 1860 sales hit 400,000 pounds, and in 1862, the same year they fed a thousand federal soldiers for a month, they still managed to sell a million pounds of wheat. The Pimas on the middle Gila River were the agricultural lords of Arizona until later in the 1860s and in the 1870s when white farmers preempted this source of their capitalist livelihood by ditching into the Gila upstream from their villages and fields. In a desert, he who controls the water controls its wealth.

Just as the Spaniards introduced an agricultural technology to the desert that was more demanding on soils and on the water-carrying capacity of rivers than had been the flood-farming, summer-cropping system of the Pimas, so were cattle a potentially devastating introduction. The only domestic animal in pre-Spanish times was the dog. The only ungulates were deer, antelope, mountain sheep, and perhaps peccaries. Their numbers were kept in check by man, natural predators, and the brutal system of balances worked out in all natural food chains.

But to Spaniards, and eventually to the Pimans among whom they were introduced, domestic livestock implied animal husbandry. Pimans hunted cattle at first, just as they had hunted deer and antelope. In time, hunting territories became cattle ranges; cattle ranges became cattle districts; and, on the Papago Reservation, cattle districts became political districts, with cattle, power, and politics becoming inextricably interwoven.

With man as an ally, livestock are given an unfair advantage over the plants and other animals in an arid environment. But the advantage may well be short-termed. Over centuries, if not over decades, human beings appear to husband domestic livestock in deserts to eventual forced removal or utter extinction.

If Spaniards were neither wary nor chary of a waste of desert resources in their farming and animal husbandry, neither were they conservationists in their architecture. They used water to make mud bricks. They sawed the tallest trees for timber in roofs. They sawed the smaller trees to burn them to charcoal to fire their lime kilns and brick kilns. They expended an enormous amount of energy — both their own and that of the desert — in erecting buildings ultimately native to Mesopotamia. They transplanted raw mud and fired mud structures to a desert where, until then, shade and shelter provided merely by brush, grass, and a few tree trunks had kept people cool in the summer and warm in winter.

So, too, did they fail to understand the value of small group mobility in the desert. Their vision of a settlement was not a *rancheria* of widely scattered houses, a *rancheria* which might be deserted part of the year while its inhabitants hunted, foraged, or farmed elsewhere. A Spanish settlement was a *pueblo* or *villa*. Villages and cities were supposed to be anchored in place; their populations were supposed to be permanent. It takes time to develop a proper system of social class, of aristocracy. Permanent buildings were necessary for such developments.

It is not correct to say that the faces of Spaniards which were once new to the northern Sonoran Desert have left. They are still here, only now they are old. And Spanish-speaking peoples remain in Pimería Alta as an important level in the stratification of human history.

Then in the mid-nineteenth century still more faces and still newer faces set foot and hoofbeat and iron-rimmed wagon wheel upon the sands. These were the Anglo-Americans. These were the sons of George Washington and Abraham Lincoln and Jefferson Davis and Robert E. Lee. These were the raggety-tailed actors in the drama of manifest destiny. These were the fulfillers of American dreams. At first, in the 1850s and 1860s, they came to the desert in dribbles. But by the end of the century they had come in droves. They came to seek mineral wealth in the desert mountains. They invaded Ajo and the Baboquivari Range. They dug holes at Cubabi and Gunsight. They spanned the desert with iron tracks linking the Atlantic Ocean to the Pacific Ocean and to the Gulf of California.

Their favorite drink was not the water-bringing and life-giving Piman wine fermented from the fruit of saguaro cactus. Neither was it mescal nor tequila from desert Agaves. It was whiskey, a staunchly Old World invention and altogether foreign to the desert. It can be taken as a kind of metaphor of the Anglo-American presence. It was a commodity which had to be imported. It totally ignored the desert, pretending none was there. Anglos used it to wash down their eastern oysters.

In the 1870s Texas drovers brought large herds of cattle into southern Arizona, replacing the vanished herds of defunct Spanish missions and haciendas. By the end of the 1870s, cattle raising, rather than hunting, gathering, and farming had become the principal means of Papago livelihood, just as the sale of wheat for cash and goods had become the major Pima livelihood.

The competition for land and water were inevitable. In 1887 the federal agent working with Papagos said:

They have been able heretofore to prosecute and carry on their cattle industry by reason of springs and water and wells at the foot of mountains, where there is fair grazing land. When the spring or well at one point becomes dry, or the grass exhausted, they drive their stock to another point, and only use their homes in villages a small portion of the year.

This small privilege is fast being wrested from them for the country is fast filling up with cattlemen (whites), and now almost at every spring or well some white man has a herd of cattle, and the inevitable result follows, the Indian is ordered to leave, and the "superior race" usually enforces such order.

On the Gila River, by the 1880s the Pimas had lost most of the surface water in their stream to white farmers who had taken the water out in upstream ditches. By 1910 it was impossible for Papagos in the Santa Cruz Valley at San Xavier del Bac to farm with surface water. Erosion in the channel had dropped the river's surface to levels far below those of their fields.

The biggest force wrought by these new Anglo-American faces, however, was not in their bigger and better ditches or in their large herds of hungry cattle. In 1896 it was reported that the white cattleman in the desert country west of the Santa Cruz basin had "sunk wells 600 to 1,000 feet in depth and [was] pumping waters therefrom. He has built great reservoirs to impound the rainwaters, and will work out his own prosperity and will develop the country if left alone."

The apple in the Garden of Eden had been chewed into. For the first time in the Sonoran Desert, vast sources of underground water had been tapped, much of it thousands of years old. The industrial revolution, with its foreign iron machines powered by fossil fuels like coal and gas and diesel and gasoline, had arrived. With this force behind him, man came to believe he could effectively ignore the desert. He could turn it as green as the tropics. He could protect himself against extremes of cold and heat. He could pretend he lived in a temperate zone where the sun shines pleasantly most of the time.

Here, truly, was a formidable force. It is the one with which we who still live in the desert are having to contend as we begin the final quarter of the twentieth century, anno Domini 1976. Two hundred years of American revolution. And we wonder whose the next faces shall be, and whether

53

their forces will be greater than those inherent in the nature of Pimería Alta.

## Bibliographic Note:

The Spaniard's description of Papagos in the Pinacate Mountains is on page 160 of Juan Mateo Manje, *Unknown Arizona and Sonora, 1693–1721*, translated by Harry J. Karns (Tucson: Arizona Silhouettes, 1954). The Papago salt expedition song is on page 173 of Frances Densmore, *Papago Music* (Bulletin 30 of the Bureau of American Ethnology, Washington, D.C.: Government Printing Office, 1929). The 1887 report of conflict between Papago and non-Indian cattlemen is by Elmer A. Howard and is published on page 6 of the *Annual Report of the Commissioner of Indian Affairs to the Secretary of the Interior for the Year 1887* (Washington, D.C.: Government Printing Office). The 1895 report of well drilling in Papago country is by Colin Cameron and appears on page 253 of the *Annual Report of the Secretary of the Interior for the Fiscal Year Ended June 30, 1896*, Vol. 3 (*Report of the Governor of Arizona to the Secretary of the Interior;* Washington, D.C.: Government Printing Office, 1896).

The most useful account of the vegetation and climate of the Sonoran Desert is in Volume 1 of Forrest Shreve and Ira Wiggins, *Vegetation and Flora of the Sonoran Desert* (Stanford, California: Stanford University Press, 1964). Data on the threefold adaptation of Upper Pimans are in Bernard L. Fontana, "Man in Arid Lands: The Piman Indians of the Sonoran Desert," in *Desert Biology*, Vol. 2, pp. 489–528, edited by George W. Brown, Jr. (New York: Academic Press, 1974). Spanish-period materials for Pimería Alta include Herbert E. Bolton, *Rim of Christendom* (New York: Russell & Russell, 1960); the Bolton-edited five-volume work, *Anza's California Expeditions* (Berkeley: University of California Press, 1930); and Francisco Garcés, *On the Trail of a Spanish Pioneer,* translated by Elliott Coues (New York: Francis P. Harper, 1900). The best single-volume description of traditional Papago culture is Ruth Underhill, *Social Organization of the Papago Indians* (New York: Columbia University Press, 1939). For Gila River Pima traditional culture, see Frank Russell, *The Pima Indians* (Tucson: University of Arizona Press, 1975).

Finally, for information about Gila River Pima subsistence based on floodwater farming, I am indebted to William Doelle and an unpublished study by him, "The Gila Pima at First Contact: 1697–1699" (ms., 1975).

# THE FIFTH WORLD—THE NINTH PLANET

## Frank Waters

❖⁖❧❧⁖❖

THE SUBJECT OF MY REMARKS HERE, "The Fifth World — The Ninth Planet," is taken from the topic of a discussion group which met last spring at Arizona State University's Conference on Teaching English and Literature. I was invited to the conference to give a talk before the general assembly, but unfortunately I was unable to attend the group meeting. I wish I had heard the discussion, for the subject has long interested me and I have written about it in my latest book.

The ninth planet in our Solar System evidently means our Earth. What the fifth world designates is not so clear, but the idea of four or five successive "worlds" on this planet goes back to antiquity. No subject would seem more vast and general than this. What relation it has to literature in the Southwest, and why a group of English teachers should have brought it up in Tempe, may seem strange. Yet the idea is very much in the air today, spreading by a curious osmosis among us all in this era of universal anxiety.

As I have mentioned, the idea of several successive "worlds" — which I take to mean land masses and whatever civilizations existed upon them — is very old indeed. A geological theory asserts that when the Earth was young there was but one great land mass that separated into two supercontinents. One was in the northern hemisphere named Laurasia, comprising what are now North America, Greenland, and Eurasia. The other, Gondwanaland, was in the southern hemisphere, joining South America, Africa, Antarctica, and other present lands. Certainly the Earth has not always presented the same outlines as it does today. Possible changes of its magnetic poles, continental drift, deep sea submergences, volcanic outbursts, glaciation, and erosion have continuously changed its face.

Various schools of esoteric theology posit four worlds or continents that successively existed in past ages before they were destroyed: the Polarian, Hyperborean, Lemurian, and Atlantean. The latter of course was the one described in Plato's *Dialogues* of the fourth century b.c. and reported to have sunk below the sea about 9500 b.c. The belief in four previous worlds was held by the ancient Greek historian Hesiod, and was embraced in the religious teachings of Zoroasterism, Hindu and Tibetan Buddhism.

The existence and location of these continental worlds have yet to be scientifically proven. Of possibly more importance is the record of four previous worlds embodied in the myths of many peoples. I am a great believer in myth. It seems to me the only true history of mankind, for it springs from the shadowy depths of our archaic human past, our collective unconscious as Jung calls it, and hence is impacted with psychological meaning. A universal language, it is expressed in archetypes, primordial thoughts or unconscious images, that rise from the unconscious into consciousness. The four previous worlds are such archetypes.

In the twenty books I have written about the Southwest over a period of forty years — so many of them concerning its Indian pueblos and tribes and their religious ceremonials — these archetypes have been of signal importance to me. They are pictorially expressed by the Navajos in their superb sandpaintings, and poetically expressed in the prayers, chants, and myth recitations of the ceremonial "sings" or "chants" which recount man's successive Emergences from each of the lower worlds to the next. Versions of this Creation Myth have been transcribed by Washington Matthews, Father Berard Haile, L. C. Wyman, and other notable scholars, and they are among the oldest native literature of the continental United States.

The same concept is held by the Pueblos, with the exception of the Hopis who believe our present world is the fourth rather than the fifth. Their Emergence to these successive worlds is the great theme informing all Hopi ceremonialism. In each of the nine great ceremonials in the annual cycle, it is reflected in recounted myths, in prayers, songs, dances, and innumerable rituals. A dramatic enactment of the Emergence from the Third World to the present Fourth World is made at Flute Spring during the Flute Ceremony. Another impressive presentation is given in the superb Niman Kachina ceremony. The chronology of the four worlds is observed by the four appearances of the masked kachina dancers during the day — at sunrise, midmorning, midafternoon, and sunset, and by their successive positions on the four sides of the plaza. The corresponding four songs they sing while dancing also recount man's occupation of each of the four worlds.

The intricacy of all these ceremonials and their rituals, so perfectly coordinated in one great pattern, is beyond the scope of these casual comments. Each of the four worlds is symbolized by a direction, North, South, West, and East; by a directional color, white, blue, yellow, and red; and by a characteristic plant and animal. Among the Hopi religious orders is the Two Horn Society whose members wear two horns symbolizing ritually remembered knowledge of the previous worlds; whereas members of the One Horn Society wear on their masks only one horn symbolizing knowledge only of the present world.

During the three years I lived on the Hopi Reservation, recording this material and its meaning from some thirty clan leaders and kiva chiefs, I was constantly amazed by its richness and abundance. It revealed a depth of spiritual perception far beyond the usual interpretations made by us of these so-called primitive and pagan native rituals. It was, in fact, a living faith validated by the great religious system that dominated all Indian America almost two thousand years ago.

Let me briefly outline the religious foundation of the pre-Columbian peoples of Mexico and Guatemala as I was enabled to explore it recently by a Rockefeller Foundation research grant. The similarities between the myths, rituals and symbols of the Nahuatl people of Mexico and those of our Southwest pueblos are markedly apparent. The Aztecs based their cosmogony and cosmology on four preceding "worlds," "eras" or "suns." Each was symbolized by a spatial quadrant, a directional color, and a distinctive plant and animal. At the end of the Fourth World a fifth was created by an assembly of gods at ancient Teotihuacan, the "Birthplace of the Gods," the greatest metropolis of Middle America and the center of its far-flung spiritual empire, whose majestic ruins are now the most awesome of all Indian America. Here was created the Fifth World or Sun, our present world, largely through the efforts of Quetzalcoatl who superceded his folk-hero role as a bringer-of-civilization by his transcendental transformation into the Lord of Dawn, the planet Venus.

This hermetic myth was transcribed from Aztec spokesmen and translated into Spanish soon after the Conquest by Fray Bernardino de Sahagún in the Florentine Codex, now translated into English by Arthur J. O. Anderson of the School of American Research and Charles E. Dibble of the University of Utah. Another ancient Aztec codex, the Codice Borgia, pictorially records it in paintings that are the most gorgeous and esoteric of all pre-Columbian America. Reproductions of them in color photoengravings were made in Rome in 1898, and interpreted by the great German scholar Eduard Seler in a two-volume commentary. It was written in German, but not translated into Spanish until 1963, and has not yet been translated into English. A sculptural depiction of the successive worlds is shown on the monumental twenty-five-ton Stone of the Sun, commonly known as the Aztec Calendar Stone. I mention these sources to illustrate how widely recorded in text, paintings, and sculpture was the multiple-world concept of the ancient Nahuas.

The same great theme was recounted by the Mayas of Yucatan and Guatemala in the *Popul Vuh, the Sacred Book of the Ancient Quiché Maya,* the oldest book of the Western Hemisphere. Its account parallels those of the Nahuas of Mexico and the Pueblos of our Southwest. The Mayas, moreover, introduced into the concept a new factor, a carefully calculated and dated chronology. Perhaps no other people on earth have been so obsessed with the notion of time. Accomplished astronomers and astrologers, they perfected about the first century B.C. the complex calendar system used throughout all Middle America, a calendar more accurate than ours today. Brilliant mathematicians, they originated the concept of zero or nought, not known until a thousand years later in India, and another thousand years later in Europe. Using a highly original and complex numbering system, they calculated time in periods ranging from twenty days to fifty-two years and cycles of 5,200 years, and these cycles they projected into the past as far as ninety million and four hundred million years.

How fantastic this seems today to us clockwatchers, programming every hour and minute of our busy day!

Of present concern here is that the Mayan priestly mathematicians and astrologers projected the beginning of their last Great Cycle to 3113 B.C. This date apparently marked the beginning of the present Fifth World after the catastrophe which destroyed the Fourth. And they predicted the present Fifth World would be destroyed by a catastrophe in A.D. 2011.

Many puzzling questions are provoked by this prediction. The classic Maya civilization held sway in the early centuries of the Christian era, long before the commonly accepted discovery of the Western Hemisphere. How then could it have nurtured the same belief in five successive worlds held in the Eastern Hemisphere? Another strange coincidence is that the ancient Shinto texts of Japan reportedly predicted our present civilization would end on the same date, A.D. 2011. It is curious too that early European astrologers like Nostradamus, who knew nothing about the Maya civilization which had been swallowed by the jungle five hundreds years before, also predicted the end of our world about A.D. 2000. And perhaps still more significant are predictions of contemporary scientific bodies that the disruption of the life-support system on this planet will occur by A.D. 2020 due to exhaustion of natural resources and pollution.

Let me interject here a note disclaiming my role as a Prophet of Doom. As I will develop later, there is a positive aspect to balance this negative view.

Yet the possibility of at least an end to our present way of life is indicated by developments here in the Southwest. There is no need to document the ravages of the technological Juggernaut destroying the land, polluting the rivers, contaminating the very air, in the name of Progress. We all know that of the flow of the mighty life-stream of the West, the Colorado, not one drop now reaches its mouth at the Gulf of California. It has been blocked by nine major dams with their hydroturbine plants, primarily to generate electric power for profitable sale. It has resulted, to name only two examples, in the useless flooding of exquisite Glen Canyon and the Navajos' sacred Rainbow Bridge. Only nation-wide public protest, sparked by the Sierra Club of California, halted the erection of still another dam in Marble Canyon which would have flooded one of the greatest natural wonders in the world — the incomparable Grand Canyon itself. There is no assurance that the Bureau of Reclamation will not renew its efforts to build the dam when public protest has died down; and more great projects are planned for the Colorado's tributaries, the Salt and Verde rivers, the Gila and San Pedro.

The electric power generated by these hydroturbine plants has not been sufficient to supply the demands by profit-hungry energy-developers backed by the Department of the Interior. So the production of more power from coal-burning plants is underway with the ruthless strip-mining of coal on the Navajos' and Hopis' sacred Black Mesa, and the colossal Four Corners power plant spewing thousands of tons of pollutants and particulates into the air. More similar projects are included in the national government's long-range plan to erect up to thirty-four coal-fired power plants, coal gassification plants, and oil shale developments throughout the upper Colorado River basin. Nor will even these be enough. Plans are under way to strip-mine the Great Plains of North Dakota, Wyoming, and Montana, notably on the Crow and Cheyenne Indian Reservations, and to erect forty-two more coal-burning plants.

There may be a rational excuse, a national excuse loudly and widely proclaimed by power-hungry developers and state leaders especially in this so-called energy crisis, for this demonic exploitation of the forces of nature for material gain. Yet it ignores a human factor. In our history of economic development we have become the richest materialistic nation in the world, but what we have gained we have paid for by loss of soul. For man's unconscious is rooted in the earth; and by ruthlessly destroying nature, we have ruptured our own inner being. We have alienated our conscious, rational selves from the maternal unconscious, the substratum of our essential being, the psychic counterpart in us of the earth itself. This split in the wholeness of the psyche Jung views as the tragedy of modern man.

The great efforts of environmental organizations are retarding to some extent the malignant growth of this mammoth industrial cancer, but they cannot stop it. For ours is a national ethic that mandates economic growth at any price. The clock cannot be turned back.

This negative view is not restricted to our Southwest, to America at large. The same imbalance between man and land, the same schism within man himself, has spread throughout the world with political unrest, economic distress, wars and revolutions, and widespread starvation. Significant indeed, as I have mentioned earlier, are the predictions of the Club of Rome and the Movement for Survival that the disruption of the life-support system on this planet will occur by A.D. 2020. This date brings us back to the date of A.D. 2011 predicted by the Mayas as the end of our present Fifth World.

It is clearly not as fantastic as it may appear. There is no doubt that we are living in a tragic period of universal doubt and despair, of drastic changes occurring too swiftly to comprehend, a period not equaled since the beginning of the Christian era, which it resembles in many ways. But now, as then, I believe we can find some hope and strength by achieving a greater perspective that will enable us to see it and ourselves more clearly. Something beyond us, and something within us, are combining to give us a new outlook and a new creativity to supercede the predictions of dire catastrophe.

In an effort to understand the constructive forces at work while rationalism and materialism speed to their end, let us look first into astrology — the preeminent science of the Mayas, and a modern science beginning to achieve the status of respectability.

The beginning of the Christian era coincided with the beginning of the zodiacal Age of Pisces, its symbol of two fish being also the symbol of Christianity. That age is now ending, and the World Clock is pointing toward an imminent hour in world history. The World Clock, as it is called, is the great 25,160-year period of the precession of the equinoxes during which the axis of the revolving earth circumscribes a circle of three hundred and sixty degrees. The circle is divided into twelve zodiacle periods of 2,160 years each, called Ages, through which the equinox passes. The end of the present Age of Pisces, the twelfth and last of the zodiacal houses, will also mark the end of the great precessional cycle of 25,160 years. Surely then, when the World Clock does strike this momentous hour, something is bound to happen — unless we deny any relationship with the greater universe of which we are a part.

What will happen, I feel, is that our nightmarish civilization will come to an end not by catastrophic destruction, but by its gradual rebirth into another conception of man's place and function on this shrinking planet — virtually an Emergence, as the Indians call it, to a new Sixth World. The deeper meaning of an Emergence may well prove to be psychological: that the mythological previous worlds of the Mayas, the Aztecs, Pueblos, and Navajos were not land masses periodically destroyed with their inhabitants, but dramatic allegories for the psychological stages on mankind's evolutionary journey from the unconscious into ever-widening consciousness. So we must look at the changes within our own psyche already taking place.

The approaching Age of Aquarius, beginning a new precessional cycle, carries the sign of the Water Bearer, and water long has been recognized as a symbol of the unconscious. Our present and unprecedented search for new values reflects our orientation inward rather than outward. The hippie movement of the past decade was an unconscious revolt of young people against our stifling materialistic ethic, a blind and unguided return to our maternal earth and a simpler way of life. Today our search inward is reaching full tide with the phenomenal public interest in psychology, particularly Jungian depth psychology. The first Jungian training institute in Zurich was founded scarcely twenty years ago; today graduate analysts are practicing in all large cities in America as well as in Europe. With this is an awakened interest in the ancient religious philosophies and metaphysical ideas of the East. Authentic texts known only to scholars a few years ago are out in mass paperback editions, crowding the shelves of newsstands, drugstores, and supermarkets; and we are flooded with an influx of Swamis, Gurus, and Yogis of all kinds. And with all this, new areas of psychic phenomena are opening up to research: extrasensory perception, telepathy, clairvoyance, mind control over matter. All these are positive signs of America's awakening from its dream of materialism.

We cannot change the world until we change ourselves; and with our growing awareness of the untapped resources of psychic energy within us, I hopefully believe we are already beginning to make our emergence to the new Sixth World of ancient mythology. What it will be, no one knows, nor how many other worlds lie ahead. We can only dimly glimpse the truth that we must rise from our present destructive level of ego-centered consciousness to a level of global harmony with all other peoples, with our common maternal earth, and finally to a harmonious relationship with the universe. What other goal can mankind have?

These conclusions are of course based on my own interpretation of the myths of Indian America. They may be questioned in detail, but their general outline seems sound. Unless we sell humanity short, it does have a future that can be anticipated without dread and fear. We are not only Southwesterners, Americans, Russians and Red Chinese, but citizens of our Solar System, of our immense Galaxy, of the infinite Universe itself. Toward this eventual realization we are now unconsciously advancing, whether we consciously realize it or not.

# BOOKS AND PEOPLE
## OF THE SOUTHWEST

*Saguaro cactus, by Dr. John P. Schaefer*

# AN AMATEUR LIBRARIAN

Paul Horgan

❧

FOLLOWING A RECOMMENDATION by his fierce but just geometry teacher, the student climbed four stories to the school library which occupied a square tower room at the top of the academic building, hoping to find that the library was open. There were no fixed library hours, and he had often come all the way up the tower only to find the door locked. Then he could only peer in longing and disappointment through the large pane of glass which was framed in the upper half of the door, and regard the shelves along the walls, and the sepia enlargements of photographic portraits of past worthies of the school faculty and regents, and hope for better luck next time.

This time, the door was open, and there was the librarian — a small, rugged, bandy-legged man with a wavy forehead curl of sandy hair which was matched in shape and color by a splendid mustache. His face was as ruddy as a crab-apple. When his principal duties allowed, he sat out the open library hours as custodian, reading *The Illustrated London News* — nostalgically, for he was a Welshman, long transplanted to America, and now the bandmaster and instructor in band instruments at the New Mexico Military Institute at Roswell. Everyone referred to him as Captain Jack. Those with an ear always knew without looking when he played a solo on the baritone horn, or sang one in the choir of St. Peter's Church in town. He was a natural musician, with a fine sense of phrasing and line — and a military sense of order.

"Excuse me, sir," said the student, "have you a copy of *Dracula*, by Bram Stoker? Major Thomas recommended it to me."

Captain Jack put down his magazine and asked cheerfully, "What color is the cover?"

"I don't know, sir."

"Then how in blazes do you expect me to find it? You go back and ask Major Thomas the color of the cover. If I find it, then you can have it."

"Yes, sir."

I went to ask — for I, a cadet, was the student looking for *Dracula* in the early 1920s — but the last class was over for that day, and so was the close order drill, and the major was gone. But I returned another day: the book was blood-scarlet, we found it, and I was captivated by elegant horror for hours.

Captain Jack was only an interim librarian. It went without saying that he had no preparation for the job — nor had the other officers who in their "free" time would keep the library open in years before and after him. But he was the only one who conceived of a system of classification, and put it into effect. The result, if bizarre in relation to subject matter, had at least the orderly virtue of keeping books together according to the colors of their bindings. The system was especially convenient for Captain Jack in shelving sets of books. I spent hours with those sets, particularly of a certain kind.

Their dominant character reflected that of the man who had left them behind when, after a period as an academic officer of the Institute, he departed under somewhat mysterious circumstances. He was an Italian — Captain Count Luigi Martini-Mancini. His sepia likeness in the library showed a slender, swarthy man with a thin pointed mustache, wearing the blue uniform. His head was turned in a genteel angle. His eyes were prominent, dark, and circled with dark-pigmented skin. He looked rather like Marcel Proust. With his minor Italian title, his aristocratic manners, and his airs of European high life, he had been a great social success in the little eastern New Mexico plains city, where his local friends used his title as a nickname, omitting the definite article when referring to him.

His legacy of books, then, had mostly to do with European royalty and aristocracy, whether in historical romances or biography — though there were sets of other fashionable fiction as well. In the absence of any current books I made my way through the historical novels of Louisa M. Muhlbach in twelve volumes, small 8vo, blue cloth, stamped in gold, with gilded tops: *Joseph the Second and His Court, Marie Antoinette and Louis XVI,* and such. I also read the collected novels of F. Marion Crawford, including

*Saracinesca, The Diva's Ruby,* and romances of grand affairs in Roman society. The novels of Eugene Sue, the Valois romances and the musketeer series of Dumas also formed part of my reading fare. These last made so great an impression on me that when I first visited the Louvre I was not in a museum, but in the vast palace whose past occupants I knew so well that it was they and their intrigues which filled the grand chambers, the corridors, alcoves, and attic dormers for me. There were plays and poems in Italian by D'Annunzio and poems of Gesue Carducci and Giacomo Leopardi, at which I stared baffled but somehow gratified. "Count" had also various single volumes which reflected his interests — *The Agony of an Empress* (anon.); the indignant memoirs of Louisa, ex-crown princess of Saxony; *Memoirs of a Diplomat's Wife,* by Mary King Waddington; a life of Leo XIII, another of Victor Emmanuel I, another of Queen Margherita, and the like. Though there was no literature in German, "Count" must have been responsible also for a splendid bronze bust of Goethe, over life-size, which gazed from a pedestal near a window overlooking the yellow brick barracks and their barren troop formation area.

If all this had no particular coherence or directly educational application, it did make reference to the larger culture and the deeper background which lay beyond the Pecos Valley; and in an isolated case now and then, such as mine, it fed that thirst for reading which, when wide choice and personal taste are not in charge, will absorb whatever is at hand rather than nothing at all.

But there were other sets which loomed eminently in Captain Jack's color classification. In the section of black bindings was a ponderous monument to culture testifying to patriotism and civic interest called *The Messages and Papers of the Presidents* in, I believe, twelve volumes. At some period after the turn of the century a salesman of awesome gifts had evidently made a killing in New Mexico, for in even moderately prosperous houses which I visited he had managed to leave behind him, for what was surely a heavy price, a set of the *Papers* as witness to the pathetic vulnerability of the householders. I doubt if a single volume of any of the presidential sets was ever opened. Certainly the one in the Institute library preserved, under a natural accumulation of dust, its mint condition.

In the blue binding section, on the other hand, was a set which held compelling interest for me. This was a ten-volume collection devoted to a photographic history of the Civil War. Here I first met Matthew Brady, and entered vicariously into the tragically moving experience of the nation and the victims of its dreadful internal struggle. The battle scenes, the bivouac landscapes, the fallen bodies, the living groups of soldiers making their

67

testament to the inquiring camera — all these had a poignancy for me which remains till this day, and I have always felt that the Civil War had been fought in an eternal autumn of lingering smoke in thickets and woods. There was another "set" whose color I cannot remember, but it was called *Battles and Leaders of the Civil War,* and I would go from the photographic history to the essays in the *Battles and Leaders* to animate in my imagination the scenes and figures of the pictures.

For the rest, the book collection, numbering perhaps fifteen hundred volumes, included familiar staples such as the works of Fenimore Cooper, Washington Irving (I remember discovering with delight his story *The Stout Gentleman*), the New England poets, the collected poems of Alice and Phoebe Cary, the novels of Dickens, George Eliot, the plays of Shakespeare, and hundreds of miscellaneous volumes, properly neglected, which had obviously been cleared out of local attics. I believe there was then no allowance for book purchases in the school budget.

But someone had authorized subscriptions to a number of periodicals. I suspect this was to answer the alert interest of Major Thomas, the mathematician, for I would see him — and usually no one else — reading *The Illustrated London News, The Literary Digest, The World's Work, The Atlantic Monthly, Scribner's Magazine, The Century Magazine, The Saturday Evening Post,* and the humorous weeklies *Life, Judge,* and *Puck.* Turning the pages of these latter, he would often chuckle in the liquid and hollow voice of the arrested tubercular; for it was tuberculosis which had brought him to New Mexico in the first place. I shared the Major's interest in these magazines, and so did my classmate, Cadet Peter Hurd, whose earliest painting style reflected a direct admiration for the reproduced work of Maxfield Parrish as it appeared in color illustrations, advertisements, and on covers.

Few enough other cadets found their way up to the fourth floor tower library. Its very location made it easy to ignore, and the academic concerns of the Institute were then confined to the classroom, so that library reference was almost never required of students. The library was mainly a symbol of what any educational institution must be able to mention, if not actually use. But limited as it was, difficult of access, neglected by the administration, it remained for me, when its few open hours coincided with my time free of classes or drill, a haven from hazing in my first cadet year; and the library habit persisted in my next two years, until I left the corps of cadets for three years in the world of music and theatre in Rochester, New York.

It was, then, with a sense of returning to a natural domain when after those three years in the East I found myself back in the tower's top room as custodian of its static collection. I had returned to New Mexico certain that I wanted to write books. I needed a job. The superintendent, Colonel J. C. Troutman, recently promoted from within the faculty, answered my random inquiry about employment with an invitation to return as full-time librarian. I accepted immediately; and then began that double activity which saw the library gradually find an ever-growing usefulness in the school, and my literary apprenticeship and my eventual public appearance as a writer.

I was as innocent of library techniques as the gallant little Captain Jack, who was grateful to have been relieved of his library duties during my absence. I set about becoming an autodidact in what was then earnestly called library science. A sophisticated faculty officer suggested that I have the school buy for me a copy of Melvil Dewey's book of his decimal classification system, and a set of the Cutter tables for author numbers, and out of the two, learn to devise call numbers. I soon began to break down the color system of my delightful predecessor, as I arranged the shelving of the meager collection according to the decimal design for classifying subject matter.

Under Colonel Troutman a modest program of acquiring current books was established; and relying on the *ALA Booklist, The Publishers Weekly, The Retail Bookseller,* and the book supplement of *The New York Times,* and with the aid of suggestions from certain faculty officers starved for new books, I ordered through a local bookstore what seemed like a feast of reading. The new book jackets of each week were pasted up on the glass pane in the library door. Cadets, too, began to glance at them. The library, under the colonel's interest, seemed to come alive in a moderate way.

In my commitment to books in all their several attractions, I established a book review periodical called *The Library* which ran for a year or so. It carried new poems (Witter Bynner, Langston Hughes, and myself, quite shamelessly), and reviews by faculty members and an occasional outsider (B. A. Botkin). The assistant editor was the cadet officer, Myron McCormick, who later became a distinguished actor. Because the library was now open on a regular schedule all day long, McCormick was granted to me also as assistant librarian. There was a feeling of growth in the school at large, which was reflected in all aspects of the library's mission.

With the addition of a junior college to the prep school years, the Institute had moved into extended educational appeal; and a separate building for the college classes was built. The ground floor end on the south was given over to the library — a generous room whose stack space alone was about the size of the old library. Further, there were basement rooms for periodical storage, and for an activity which McCormick and I set up. This was a book bindery. We were both interested in the fine trade bindings issued by Alfred A. Knopf, and we sought to reflect their decorative innovations in book design. We learned how binding was done by tearing a book apart and reassembling it. We received as a gift a book press, brass die tools, various clamps, and other equipment for the binding of books. Teaching other cadet assistants what we had learned, we did almost all of our own re-binding in the basement of Willson Hall at a great saving in cost. (Heavy reference books and periodicals were too much for us — these were sent away for professional treatment.) We bought fine stocks of binding cloth — buckram, airplane linen, vellum — in bright colors; and when the rebound books were pressed and dried out, I went to work adding the titles and authors to their spines, always supported by various decorative flourishes applied in gold or colored leaf with a hot electric stylus.

In due course, following the move to the new library, we were permitted to keep open hours after the night study hall, and our need for desk assistants grew until we had ten or twelve cadets on part-time jobs. The move entailed the purchase of new furniture and stacks. It was a fine time of shopping by catalogue. The results impressed visitors, who could be told that our metal stacks were made by the Sneed Company of New Jersey, and were identical to some lately installed in the newly renovated Vatican Library. The tables and chairs of the reading room space were of heavy pale oak in a handsome design. By what stratagems I do not recall I was able to induce a new superintendent (who was not so sensitive to books and libraries as his predecessor Colonel Troutman) to authorize the purchase of the complete Oxford English Dictionary in magnificent red and gold leather bindings at a cost of almost eight hundred dollars. For this we designed a special case to match the rest of the new furniture. It had a glass front which had to be unlocked with a key kept at the loan desk. It was the library's special treasure, and the bronze bust of Goethe seemed to find it a fitting complement for his noble presence.

Our book budget was increased to a hundred dollars a month, which after our previous ration seemed princely. There was a catch — every list which I prepared for purchase had to be personally examined and approved by the colonel. There were sometimes questions, but on the whole, he let the list stand, and after a while he did not bother to go over it. Our acquisitions grew according to faculty requests, the offerings of the book season, and my own taste; for I felt certain that any book which would interest me must surely appeal to others. A fine interest in new books took hold in the cadet corps, and we gave excitement to this by limiting the new books to a circulation of one week. For these I drew pictures on the card pockets inside the front cover, suggesting something of the contents much as a publisher's jacket often did. There must have been hundreds of these little pocket drawings, dashed off at my desk with black and colored India inks and pasted in the books as the last item of their preparation for release. Lawrence Clark Powell acquired a sizeable collection of these which I believe he lodged in the UCLA Library, and Peter Hurd has another batch of them and, to my half-irritated gratification, many of the book pockets were torn out and stolen by cadet borrowers who seemed to like them, for I would often see them later pinned up as decorations in cadets' rooms during my evening tours of duty as study hall officer.

We began to keep circulation statistics which showed a continuing rise in library use. The ground floor accessibility of the library had much to do with this, and so did its new atmosphere, the general air of club-like comfort we sought to maintain, and our various improvised ways to give the library an individual and appealing character.

All this was useful; but we still lacked high technical finish in our procedures, and it was with relief and gratitude that we were able to add an expertly trained cataloguer to the staff who steadily created a first-class card catalogue of our holdings. This was Constance Coiner, the wife of an army officer assigned to the department of military science and tactics by the War Department. Mrs. Coiner was pretty and witty, in addition to being a trained librarian; and the presence of a young and charming woman in the hitherto all-male library greatly appealed to the cadet population.

For me, with my lack of technical training, it was reassuring to have professional qualifications added to the staff. I felt more comfortable about taking full advantage of the generous arrangement granted to me by the superintendent, Colonel Pearson, under which I could work at my writing every morning from nine-thirty to eleven-thirty in the bindery, "provided" such a schedule did not interfere with the performance of my overall duties as librarian. Under this program, my early books were written; and at the same time, the library seemed to maintain its steady development as a lively element of the school's whole character. I do recall, though, with rueful humor, that a comment on my daily absence was wittily made by someone unknown who had evidently persisted in looking for me. I had made a placard with which to caption a changing exhibit we offered from our tiny store of relatively rare books. Placed on a glass case containing the exhibited item, it read, "The Rarity of the Week." One day, in that slightly hazy state which follows a morning's writing, I returned from the bindery to my desk in a far corner of the stacks and found that someone had taken the little sign from the exhibit case and placed it on my desk, making me "The Rarity of the Week."

Schools and colleges were annually inspected by formidable teams of academic persons on behalf of the association whose duty it was to encourage high educational standards. Accreditation depended on the favorable findings of such teams. The Institute came under the North Central Association of Schools and Colleges. After our annual inspection one year, which the Institute passed as usual, another team, evidently on the recommendation of the Association, came from the Carnegie Corporation to inspect the library, with a view to determining whether we deserved the grant of $5,000 for the purchase of reference works which the Foundation was bestowing that year on various institutions. The examiners came. They grilled, combed, tested, weighed, noted, were impassively polite, and departed. In a short time we heard that we would receive the grant. It was a splendid opportunity — the single most significant leap forward in the library's history up to that point. Using the recommended list of titles published by the Corporation, we set about systematically spending our $5,000 for what became the extended core of the reference collection.

With acquisitions under this grant, and our regular rate of accessions, we were rapidly outgrowing our stack space. Captain Jack's little nucleus of 1,500 variegated and color-matched volumes was now almost lost in a collection ten times as large or more; and the regents and administration of the Institute began to think, I suppose with my prompting, about a third library to be newly built.

By now I had been long committed to a sense of vocation as a librarian. My delight in the materials of the job seemed directly to enrich my whole life as a bookman who wrote books. I was lucky that my work as both writer and custodian/circulator of books gave me deep satisfaction and fulfillment. It was therefore a further joy to be active in helping to plan a new library.

I went to work designing a new building in all its functional aspects, refraining, with difficulty, on the whole, from indicating detailed aesthetic architectural features. I sent for and studied the admirable plans and sections of the Baker Library at Dartmouth, and I almost memorized James T. Gerould's *The College Library Building, its Planning and Equipment* (Scribner, 1932). I was delighted when in the form of the first sketches from the Institute's architects my general scheme for the new building was visible — but with an important modification: for my concept gave the whole building to the library, while the school authorities along with the architects gave the library only one half of the building, the other half being devoted to the administrative offices of the Institute. Still, by envisaging a plan perhaps grandiose for its time, I was lucky to obtain for the library a new plant many times larger than its then current size, and spaces for functions such as special collections, browsing, and seminar rooms which we had never had before.

The situation of the building was felicitous — behind the flagpole, and facing the main part of the Institute. Symbolically, as tenant of half of the building, the library was now on a par with the school's highest administrative functions; and radii from all of the school's activities led to that central place. We were to occupy two whole floors, together with a fine second story room in the high tower at the middle of the building. In its physical prominence, then, and its new facilities and comforts, the library took its greatest step forward as a visibly vital constituent of the educational process.

By the first definition of *amateur* in the OED, I was in the fullest sense an amateur — *one who loves or is fond of; anyone who has a taste for anything*. However, my known deficiency in technical preparation for my post, excepting that which my working experience had taught me, led to a certain amount of uneasiness, let us charitably say, among a few faculty colleagues, and in fact, may have made my status on the record somewhat detrimental to the Institute's position in official reports to accrediting agencies and the like. The OED's second definition of amateur might be seen as representing this view — *dabbler, or superficial student or worker*. In any case, it was thought prudent to engage another full-time librarian who held all the requisite credentials and skills which would satisfy any official inquiries about our professionalism. This was Raymond W. Douglas, whom I welcomed at the train on his arrival in Roswell as my new assistant librarian. Curiously enough, he had been engaged without my knowledge; I was told only after the fact that he was to come. It was therefore a discouraging shock for both of us to learn that the premise of his appointment was misunderstood by us both. His dismay was increasingly visible at the meal with which I welcomed him, for he had been officially informed that he was to replace me, while I had been allowed to believe that he joined us to work directly under me. With obvious chagrin he made clear to me the terms of his appointment, and could hardly believe, any more than I could, that I had never been told what they were.

As soon as I could I went to the superintendent to learn the actual position. It appears that Douglas was right in his expectation of becoming head librarian. In the showdown, the colonel seemed unable to explain to me why I had not been notified of this, and the matter ended with his confirming me in my post, with Douglas as assistant. The arrangement was supremely awkward in its inception and for some time in its effect. Douglas remained, though in an unhappy frame of mind. Gradually, however, he overcame his disappointment, became friendly, and brought excellent professional practice and many useful innovations to our operation. One of the latter was a delightful pamphlet he composed which was to inform all new cadets in their orientation week of how to use the library. For this, Douglas asked me to draw little marginal illustrations. The booklet had a fine success, and our collaboration in this and other affairs led the way to harmony. After a couple of years with us, he departed to found and direct the library school at the University of Texas in Austin, where some years later we had a convival reunion.

In the new building, I remained as librarian until the onset of the Second World War. In the meantime, despite my technical shortcomings, I had been approached by two universities to become director of libraries, and by a distinguished college for women to be its librarian. But it was clear that none of the three positions would allow me time to write as generously as my arrangement with the Institute, in its lesser scale of demands; and I elected to remain, happy with the new building, and getting on with my books, of which, by 1942, I had published my first dozen or so.

But with the onset of the War, I asked for leave of absence in order to join the Army, which was granted. Thus my career as a librarian came to an end. Upon my return from military service I was asked to become assistant to the president, General Hugh M. Milton, a post I kept for only half a year. I was the fortunate holder of a Guggenheim Fellowship for writing, and I was eager to resume work on a history of the Rio Grande which I had scarcely begun before the war. General Milton considerately released me from my contract, and again I took up my literary concerns, now full time, to begin the long labors in search of what amounted to a second, and separate, literary reputation. This was more difficult than it might have been if, at the outset of the War, I had not agreed to the melting down of the plates of all my pre-war books in order to help supply metal for war effort. Thus, such continued circulation as my books might have had otherwise during my absence from authorship was interrupted, and by the time I was again publishing, a new generation of writers, readers, and reviewers had come of age, to whom my work was, except in anthologies, relatively unknown. *Great River* required ten years of research and writing after the War. With it in 1954 I made my second debut, now as a historian. Since then, my books have appeared fairly regularly year by year.

Since my departure from the Institute library, it has grown and flourished as never before. In post-war years, the book collection, I understand, has reached a figure of approximately sixty thousand — a creditable figure for a non-university student body of presently about eight hundred. Highly motivated and well-prepared librarians have headed the staff in turn, and professional staff members have been consistently retained. The need for additional stack space led to excavation of rooms below the library. Modifying improvements have been made throughout the building. More than ever the library is the hub of the academic philosophy and program of the prep and junior college courses. The acquisitions policy is more than sufficient — it is generous. Under highly able current leadership the library's resources are available for the first time to the community of Roswell to parallel the advantages of the city's public library. Forty-five years after the search for *Dracula* in its red binding in a remote tower room four stories above the drill formation area, the library of the New Mexico Military Institute, meeting various stages of need, and guided by successive staffs who responded to those stages with devoted imagination, goes forward in energetic maturity.

If there were a graceful way out of noting one more fact in this sketch about the library, I would take it, for to say what comes next must surely sound self-serving; yet to omit it would seem indifferent to an honor given me by the Institute in a recent year. Though I was too diffident to be present at dedicatory ceremonies and instead was represented by my brother (who preceded me as a cadet), I must shamelessly but in deep gratitude record that the Institute library now bears my name.

# "GIVE THIS PLACE A LITTLE CLASS";
## THE SAGA OF A DESERT RAT
### Ward Ritchie

∴ঙ৪∴

IT WAS SOME FORTY YEARS AGO that I first met Harry Oliver. He looked then much as he did in his last years, perhaps a little younger but not noticeably so. He had already created an image for himself, as any imaginative motion picture art director could, and had expertly moulded himself into it.

The Ward Ritchie Press was then on the eastern fringe of Hollywood in a rather poetic sounding location — on Hyperion Avenue between Lyric and Fountain Avenues. The Walt Disney Studios were but a few blocks up the street and we enjoyed an ever-vibrant association with their crazy, creative artists and writers. We also had a pleasant relationship with the Metro-Goldwyn-Mayer Studios. They had at one time photographed our pressroom when it was located on Griffith Park Boulevard, a few blocks away. They built a similar pressroom on their studio lot for a picture they were shooting and from time to time they would borrow our Washington hand press and other equipment for pictures in which they were showing an old-time printing shop.

I don't remember, after these many years, how I first came to meet Harry Oliver. It may have been through one of these associations, but I do remember that I was impressed by his reputation and accomplishments. Since he was born in the month of April in the year 1888 he must have been forty-nine or fifty years old at that time. I was well aware that as one of the outstanding art directors in Hollywood he had won two Oscars — one for the

*Seventh Heaven,* which featured Janet Gaynor and Charles Farrell, and the second for *Street Angel.*

Harry was born in Minnesota, amongst the lakes. His boyhood friends were trappers, woodsmen and rivermen. He was a dropout from school after the sixth grade because his ever-fluid mind couldn't adapt itself to conventional spelling and he saw no purpose in continuing. Even though he couldn't spell, he could draw beautifully and accurately. He spent some time posting bills for Ringling Brothers Circus before becoming a screen painter for a theater in Minneapolis. Gradually he was drawn west and to Hollywood to create motion picture sets. Many will still remember Harold Lloyd's hair-raising escapades when he was forever perilously dangling from great heights. Harry had built a set hanging over the entrance to the Second Street tunnel in downtown Los Angeles for an Irwin Willet picture. It was so imaginatively spectacular that both Harold Lloyd and Hal Roach subsequently used it to thrill their movie public.

On the day we met, Harry Oliver and I drove to Los Feliz Boulevard in Glendale to have lunch at the Tam-O'Shanter, possibly the most picturesque restaurant in Southern California at that time. Nature must be given some credit for the attractiveness of the waitresses there, but Oliver had enhanced their natural beauty with the Scottish costumes he had designed for them. The restaurant itself, with its hand-hewn beams, its huge stone fireplace, old sea chests and leaded-bottle windows was also his creation.

Over a plate of ground round steak with chili and beans we talked about a manuscript which he had brought for my consideration. In 1932 he had built for the San Diego Fair a twenty-one acre "Gold Gulch" attraction with saloons, dance hall girls, running streams for gold panning and all of the imaginative allurements of the early West. He loved the history and the romance of the arid lands of the Southwest. On first coming to California he had built for himself an adobe house in the district of Palms, with six-foot walls surrounding it. There he lived with his family for some twenty years. Also he homesteaded a place in the Borrego Valley and moulded adobe bricks to build another home, which clinched his love for the California desert.

The 1930s were severe years. Hardly anyone I knew had much money but it didn't seem to bother us. There was a great camaraderie. A gallon of wine could be had for thirty cents and all shared. Our printing shop was a focal spot where most of the local artists and writers would gather. We'd have parties, gab fests and sketch classes with equally poverty-affected models almost every night. The habitués included Fletcher Martin, Delmer Daves, George Stanley (who by the way designed the "Oscar"), Paul Land-

77

acre, Archibald Garner, Gordon Newell, Barse Miller and Lawrence Clark Powell, who came to gaze, rarely to draw. It was a time of almost complete poverty of which we were almost unaware. We shared and enjoyed the days together.

I had been printing books for several years, selling barely enough copies to pay for the paper and ink. We didn't seem to be bothered with income and sales taxes and every book that was sold added a bean to the pot. Oliver had written what he called a "Haywire History of the Borrego Desert." He also made innumerable woodcuts and drawings to illustrate it. Whether he convinced me to publish the book or I enticed him into letting me do it I don't remember. But we did publish the book with the title of *Desert Rough Cuts.* Anyone finding a copy of this book nowadays will see that we found a paper on which to print it that looks as if it had been out in the desert sun, and the many decades since its publication have added patina. It is an amusing book, suggesting the wise humor that was to emanate from this man in the years to follow. In his introduction he wrote, "It is to you, my dear posterity, whether you're born yet or not, that I want to tell about the desert prospectors, who, with only their burros, prowled this desert thinking out their problems close to nature and far away from confusion. So I ask you to put in a few commas or take a second shot on anything I've written and try to get at what I'm a'sayin'."

I have also forgotten how many copies we printed of this book. Not too many I recall, certainly not enough to help either of us financially. Harry still had his adobe house in Borrego on the 160 acres he had homesteaded. He needed cash and offered it to me for $300. At the time there was nothing I could have wanted more, but I couldn't even afford the gasoline to visit the place. I presume it was lost, for at that time with only five dollars in his pocket he bought a cheap bottle of whiskey and in his 1929 Model "A" station wagon headed out alone for a new life on "his" desert.

It was many decades before I was to see Harry Oliver again. I would occasionally see copies of his *Desert Rat Scrap Book,* but for his life during those intervening years I have had to glean from the recollections of his eldest daughter, Ann Fern Oliver Deily and articles about him I had scavenged from *Westways* and the Los Angeles *Times.*

His daughter wrote of those first vagabond desert years, "He ran a string of burros for the Forest Service and for a year wrote a desert column for fifteen California and Arizona papers. He kept working until he saved one hundred dollars with which he bought a piece of land in Thousand Palms, continuing working and making adobe bricks on Sundays. In two years there were enough bricks. Fort Oliver was built and into it he moved. The small house beside the road held little besides a bed, a stove, some ancient type, a bureau, a broken mirror and a couple of dilapidated chairs. He always said that he had a 'one bedroom with path' (there never was a bathroom added — too much involved!).

"There he lived, the two-time Oscar winner, with a dog named Whiskers, two cats, a crow, a tortoise and a roadrunner. His beloved burros lived in the hills and fed themselves. He was a happy man. Having little or no money, he wore dead men's shoes saved for him by a cobbler in Indio. For food he was sustained principally by dates given him by workers in the nearby groves."

In 1946 he wrote, illustrated and had printed what he called a five-page newspaper, "the only one in America you can open in the wind." He peddled it around the desert for a thin dime a copy until he realized that it cost him twenty-five cents to produce it. Supposedly it was a quarterly publication but it actually appeared when Oliver's mood and inclination to work were in conjunction. For most of these years he claimed that he printed it on an old Washington hand press now in the library of the California State University at Fullerton. He wrote most of the copy, probably all of it, cut his illustrations by lamplight, since the old Fort didn't have electricity. He maintained that he printed every day when he wasn't out peddling copies, haunting the desert or carrying on his crusade to preserve it.

This hand press, which is similar in operation to those on which most early printing was done, caught his eye in 1946 in the plant of the Inland Engraving and Colortype Company in San Bernardino. More modern mechanical equipment had long since supplanted the primitive hand press, but at that time engraving plants occasionally still used them for pulling proofs. Oliver, still an art director at heart, envisioned this hand press in his adobe with him printing the *Desert Rat Scrap Book* on it. For some years he had been scavenging job printing shops around the desert, picking up battered fonts of antique type faces, and now he wanted a press to complement them. His cajoling was successful and he was allowed to move the press to his place in Thousand Palms on perpetual loan.

What a love for labor this labor of love must have elicited during the next few years. Oliver always intimated that he printed the 10,000 copies of each of his *Desert Rat Scrap Book* on this hand press. This probably was another of his "tall tales." The hand press requires great physical effort to operate. Each impression must be pulled vigorously by a muscular man, and to print such a large sheet as the *Scrap Book* would probably take the strength of two men. Each time the type must be inked by hand, a sheet of paper placed into position, the bed of the press rolled under the platen and

79

an impression pulled. It is slow, tedious work. It is estimated that when John Gutenberg was printing his *Bible* around the year 1450 he managed to complete about one hundred sheets an hour with the assistance of a shopful of helpers.

Oliver's hand press was over seventy years old, having been made in Chicago in 1870. The Washington hand press on which I started printing in 1932 was also an old one and I liked to suggest that it had come from the Mother Lode where Mark Twain had printed on it. I think that Harry Oliver was at least as honest as I. He, however, was able to create a creditable pedigree for his press. The following account was gathered from the *Inyo Register* on Thursday, June 22, 1950.

"The first fifteen years of its history is still in limbo. In 1885 or 1886 it appeared in Calico where it was used to turn out the boom camp's newspaper, the *Calico Print*. Fire was the fate of so many early California printing presses, but this one survived the Calico fire of 1887 with only its wooden handle and leather straps damaged. It was repaired and printed a post-fire edition on the only material still available, some singed paper scraps and bed sheets. When Calico boomed and more modern equipment was brought in, the old press went to Needles where F. H. Barberd brought out the first issue of *Our Bazoo* in October 1888. He sold out to a man named Booth and the paper became *Booth's Bazoo* and eventually, and quite logically, *The Needles Eye*. The hegira of the press continued to Tonopah, Greenwater, Candelaria and Bullfrog before ending up unheralded and unwanted in a second-hand printers' supply house in Los Angeles." It was bought by the San Bernardino Engraving Company as a back-up proof press in the 1920s, but was virtually unused for twenty years until Oliver loaded all its eight hundred pounds into his ancient station wagon and deposited it in his adobe to reactivate it with loving pride.

In addition to the old press, the antique type, and the printing which he did on any discarded paper he could find, Harry Oliver decorated the walls of his adobe with the sometimes tragic trifles discarded on the desert by earlier travelers which he had picked up during his wanderings over a quarter of a century. There were steam irons and crimping irons, trappings of women's continuing vanity that at some time had been reluctantly abandoned, together with cooking utensils, pack saddles, water barrels — relics of hope and despair from earlier desert travelers. Seldom would he return from his frequent wanderings without bringing something he had found. But in recompense he "salted" the desert with lure for others who might come out seeking sun-colored bottles, oxen's skulls and bleached wagon wheels. He carved hundreds of peg legs and scattered them over the desert for the inevitable amateur prospectors who were still searching for the fabled "Lost Peg Leg Mine."

A familiar and beloved character with an ever-present pipe, a jutting vandyke and white locks hanging from under his black Stetson, Oliver became the emperor and protector of the desert region around Palm Springs. He'd walk miles picking up trash. He printed signs reading, "Shame! look at what you did. Beauty was here before you came," and placed them on debris heaps. He once commented, "The land is so full of wildflowers this Spring you can't even see the beer cans." When a sheepherder brought a large flock into the Coachella Valley and cut a wide swath through the millions of blooms, Oliver created so much stir through his writing to the newspapers that the Board of Supervisors were finally forced to oust the sheep to enforce their ordinance prohibiting the gathering of wildflowers.

Eventually, because of age he packed as many of his mementoes as he could and moved to the Motion Picture Home in Woodland Hills where he lived the rest of his life. Old Fort Oliver was empty but not wholly neglected. People were continuously stopping by to inspect it and photograph it, hauling away whatever they could pick up. Deserted, stripped by vandals and aged by buffeting sand storms, it has become almost what he had originally intended it to be. He had said, "I wanted to build an authentic one-hundred-year-old outpost, not to fool anybody, you understand, but to give this place a little class."

He also wrote, "Any legend is just another lie that has attained the dignity of age." Certainly Harry Oliver attained the dignity of age and became a legend in his time. When visitors questioned the authenticity of some of his claims, he would shrug his shoulders, smile and reply, "If you can't get anything else from the desert, you'll develop a sense of humor.'"

His insight was keen and he had an apt way of expressing his philosophy.

"Worry is like a rocking chair: It gives you something to do when you ain't going anywhere."

"To avoid trouble breath through the nose. It keeps the mouth shut."

"The wisest owl occasionally hoots at the wrong time."

"The records show that the tortoise won only one race with the hare."

"Animals are smart — horses never bet on people."

"It don't take backbone to belly up to a bar."

"One of the greatest labor saving devices of today is mañana."

And as he finally sums it up:

"To be a nice old man is stupid. These years in the hermit business have been happy years. Never miss a chance to make someone happy, even if you have to leave him alone to do it."

# RICHARD J. HINTON
# AND THE AMERICAN SOUTHWEST

Harwood P. Hinton

✦❧✦

ON A LATE SPRING DAY in 1877, a short middle-aged man with a full beard and shoulder-length hair stepped off the stage at Prescott, Arizona Territory. The traveler wore a smartly tailored suit and walked with a jaunty air. He spoke with a distinct cockney accent, reflecting his English birth, and conducted his affairs in a business-like manner. His arrival was expected, for the Prescott *Miner* had informed its readers that Colonel Richard J. Hinton, managing editor of the San Francisco *Evening Post,* was preparing a handbook to Arizona and would shortly visit the principal towns of the territory. Hinton's stay in Prescott was brief. He talked with the local newspaper editors, mining engineers, and other informed persons, then departed for California.

Few in Prescott knew that an internationally known journalist had been in their midst — a journalist whose career had touched many of the major events and issues of the time. In the 1850s Hinton had fled England as a young political radical, entered the newspaper trade in New York, and joined abolitionist John Brown in Kansas; in the following decade he wrote Lincoln's campaign biography, mustered and commanded black troops in the Union Army, and became one of the first Marxists in the United States. The Southwest was not new to him. In 1858 he had visited Colorado and New Mexico gathering information for a handbook to the Pikes Peak region, published the following year. His projected handbook to Arizona, however, would surpass the earlier work in sales and as a promotional tract.

Although little known today, Richard Hinton deserves a prominent place among those who traveled, described, and interpreted the American Southwest during the closing decades of the nineteenth century.

Hinton was a native of England, born in London on November 25, 1830. Following in his father's footsteps, he entered the stone cutter's trade, but his restless mind soon drew him in other directions. Hinton's father was a labor leader, and young Richard early shared his interest in expanding the rights and opportunities of the working man. He read omnivorously, took courses in shorthand and printing at a mechanics institute, and joined the Chartists, a political group who were demanding Parliamentary reforms for the laboring classes. When the British government outlawed this radical party, Hinton sailed for America in 1850 to avoid arrest.

In New York City, Richard found employment in a printing shop and spent his free time polishing his shorthand skills and taking engineering drawing courses at Columbia University. In 1854 he obtained a position as a newspaper reporter. Sent to Boston to cover a meeting called by abolitionist Theodore Parker, Hinton was caught up in the rhetoric and fervor to free the black from bondage. Shortly thereafter, with several companions, he raided a Boston jail in an attempt to release a man accused of violating the Fugitive Slave Act. He also met Walt Whitman, promoted the poet's new book, *Leaves of Grass,* and attended abolitionist rallies with him. Leaving New York, Hinton joined the staff of the *Boston Traveler,* and quickly became a disciple of Wendell Phillips, whose inflammatory preaching fixed the young Englishman's views on the slavery issue.

In June of 1956, Hinton joined a band of men taking arms and ammunition to the free soil settlers in Kansas. The town of Lawrence had been sacked by a pro-slave group and a civil war was in the offing. Ostensibly Hinton was a correspondent of the *Traveler,* but en route west he stopped at the office of the *Chicago Tribune* and engaged to supply news for that organ, too. While in Chicago, he also met John C. Fremont, the Republican candidate for President. The crisis in Kansas had passed when Hinton's group arrived, but he decided to stay in that frontier territory. Besides forwarding copy to a half dozen Eastern newspapers, he soon was engaged in launching newspapers supporting the new Republican party.

In 1858, Hinton and several other English-born journalists in Kansas pledged their support to the militant John Brown. A year later, when Brown was arrested for seizing the Harper's Ferry arsenal, Hinton conspired with a group to rescue him. Brown heard of the plot and forbade it. Hinton then joined English journalist James Redpath in writing a biography of Brown. For weeks they labored day and night in a Boston apartment on the project, hoping it would explain and justify his actions. On Christmas Day, 1859, twenty-three days after their hero was hanged for treason, they delivered the manuscript to a publisher. Their book helped create the legend and myth that eventually surrounded Brown's tragic role in American history. It also illustrated the young journalist's keen interest in capitalizing on the main chance for a good story.

Hinton's experiences during the 1860s were equally varied and interesting. A Republican stalwart, he went east and offered his pen to party leaders, first to write a campaign biography of William H. Seward, and then of Abraham Lincoln. In both cases the authorship was anonymous because of his ties with John Brown. He interviewed Lincoln at length, and published his biography in May of 1860. It sold 10,000 copies within two weeks. Ironically, Hinton was no admirer of Lincoln, feeling that the Illinois politician's position on abolitionism was very weak. With the outbreak of war, Hinton returned to Kansas and pressed Senator James Lane and others for a commission to raise black troops. When authorization came in late 1862, Hinton spearheaded the muster of the First Regiment Kansas Colored Volunteers. He served with black troops on the Missouri border and wrote a book about General Sterling Price's Confederate invasion of that district. Hinton also held staff positions in Kansas and Arkansas; later in Tennessee he was a district inspector for the Freedman's Bureau. In 1865 he was mustered out of service with the rank of brevet lieutenant colonel.

Hinton returned to newspaper work in Washington for a while, then began seeking government jobs. In 1867 he wrangled an appointment as Commissioner of Emigration in Europe and went abroad where he visited with the leading Socialists in England and on the continent, and historian-economist Karl Marx, who reinforced his views on working class problems. Upon returning to the United States the veteran journalist became the Washington representative of the Internationale movement. Most of Hinton's subsequent career involved either newspaper work or government service. In these roles, he visited the American Southwest on repeated occasions.

Hinton's first excursion into the Southwest occurred in the fall of 1858 as a Kansas newspaperman. The recent discovery of gold in the Pike's Peak region of western Kansas (later Colorado) had caused a rush of argonauts to the new El Dorado, and Hinton joined this migration to obtain information for a guidebook. On the trip he busily jotted down information on stage routes, expenses, and traveling conditions. Then with James Redpath, he produced a pocket-sized volume entitled *Hand-book to Kansas Territory and the Rocky Mountains' Gold Region; accompanied by Reliable*

*Maps and a Preliminary Treatise on the Preemption Laws of the United States.* The book was published in New York City in 1859. Unlike the dozen or so others preparing Pikes Peak guidebooks that year, Redpath and Hinton directed their volume to the Easterner who planned to go west and seek his fortune in the gold fields.

The *Hand-book to Kansas Territory* was three and three-quarters by five and three-sixteenths inches in size and contained 177 pages. It was divided into two parts. Part one provided general information on the sprawling territory, and gave advice on routes and transportation facilities. Included also were a bibliography of books on Kansas, a list of newspapers published there, and a roster of towns and counties. The authors encouraged young people and artisans to emigrate, but warned the professional class — doctors, lawyers, ministers, gamblers, and politicians — that the mines already were crowded. Goldseekers were urged to purchase a stout trunk for the trip, one that would survive a drop from a three-story house. Part two of the guidebook focused on the Pike's Peak mines. It discussed their history and locations, and gave hints on dealing with local Indians. The appendices carried pre-emption laws, business ads and two maps — one of the Kansas-Nebraska country and the other derived from Lt. G. K. Warren's recent military survey. Because of its positive advice to emigrants and its promotion in the East, the book sold well.

Hinton did not venture west again for over fifteen years. Then, in 1876, he went west to work as a reporter for the San Francisco *Evening Chronicle.* Several months later he became managing editor of the *Evening Post.* Here, Colonel Hinton (he now began using his military title) met Henry George, former editor of the *Post* and a kindred spirit. George was promoting his unique single tax theory and crusading against increasing industrialism in the nation.

In California, Hinton found that there was a great deal of interest in the mines in neighboring Arizona Territory. A number of businessmen had invested there and were spurring the Southern Pacific Railroad to extend its tracks from California east into what, economically speaking, was a colony of the Golden State. Transportation access would enhance the development of known mines and speed prospecting for new deposits. Either through design or assignment, Hinton began collecting information for a pocket-sized handbook on Arizona. He read the few standard works on the territory, and in the spring of 1877 set out on a tour of the "coming country."

Hinton traveled by train to Yuma, and there boarded a stagecoach, following close on the heels of a railroad survey crew making a route across southern Arizona. Moving east along the Gila, he turned south up the Santa Cruz, visiting such places as Tucson, Tubac, San Xavier, and Ajo. Leaving the settlements behind, he also journeyed east to the San Pedro River and Fort Bowie in the Chiricahua Mountains. From there Hinton went north to Phoenix and Prescott. A "boomer" spirit was strong everywhere. Government officials, local merchants, and newspapermen were eager to help him with his handbook. At each major town, Hinton engaged an agent to collect information and sell subscriptions to his book. He also wanted photographs, engravings, and maps to serve as illustrations. He made a major effort to be resourceful and thorough. Working rapidly Hinton delivered a completed manuscript to the publishers only a matter of months after he had begun it.

Hinton's work, entitled *The Hand-book to Arizona: Its Resources, History, Towns, Mines, Ruins, and Scenery,* was published early in 1878. It was a joint venture by Payot, Upham & Company of San Francisco and the American News Company of New York. The little pocketbook had soft covers and measured four and seven-eighths by seven and three-eighths inches. The front cover carried the title, *The Resources and Natural Wealth of Arizona,* while a shorter title, *Natural Wealth of Arizona,* appeared on the spine. Small and fat (600 pages), the volume had only seven pages of business advertisements; subsequent printings carried up to forty pages of ads. Hinton placed illustrations in most of the chapters (including a Spanish map of the Southwest made in 1777), and provided the reader a large (twenty-four by thirty-four and one-half inches) fold-out map of Arizona Territory. The purpose of the book, the author stated in the preface, was to satisfy "a growing want" for information about Arizona by prospectors, emigrants, travelers, and tourists. A decade later, historian Hubert H. Bancroft stated that Richard Hinton's *Hand-book* compared "very favorably with the works of the better class relating to other parts of the country."

The *Hand-book* contained nineteen topical chapters. The opening chapters introduced the reader to Arizona, described the various ways to reach the territory, and reviewed its recent history and singular physical and geological features. Two chapters presented a valuable survey (by county) of mines, mills and mining districts. The reader also was taken on a trip from Yuma to the Santa Cruz Valley to Fort Bowie. The remaining half of the book touched on such general topics as towns, agriculture, the military, climate, flora and fauna, Indians, Spanish explorations, and ancient ruins. The text contained liberal quotes from newspapers, speeches, articles, and books. The appendix included mining and land laws, a list of Territorial officials, and miscellaneous data. The concluding section was a business directory (by town), glossaries, drawings of mining equipment, and a bibliography of sources consulted. There was no index.

Although basically a promotional tract for the Southern Pacific Railroad, Hinton's *Hand-book* unexpectedly became a best-seller. The discovery of the Tombstone mines caused a rush into Arizona, and the book was in sudden demand. It went through several reprintings in hardback. Hinton copyrighted the guide in his name, but it is doubtful that he realized substantial royalties from its sale. Whatever he obtained was quickly dissipated, for he was a notorious spender.

By the early 1880s, Richard Hinton had left California and re-entered government service. This period probably was the nadir of his career. Employed as a special customs agent by the Treasury department, he began shuttling between Nogales and El Paso to investigate rustling and smuggling on the Mexican border. This traveling was not entirely a waste of time, for his journalistic instinct kept him alert to the country and he later wrote articles about his experiences. During this period Hinton briefly became embroiled in El Paso politics. Agreeing to help edit the newly launched El Paso *Times,* he provoked a furor when he ran an article intimating that a reporter for the competing *Lone Star* had been involved in a recent murder in the tenderloin district. Simon H. Newman, editor of the *Lone Star,* lashed out at the colonel, calling him a "moral assassin" and a lying villain and threatened to "expose" his past. Anticipating unpleasant reactions if his Kansas and Civil War activities were aired, Hinton quietly withdrew from the *Times* staff. In 1884 he completed his Treasury assignment and was shifted to the Department of Agriculture to work on special projects.

In the late 1880s Hinton became involved in on-going government studies of the arid West. Increasing interest in the Western states over problems of drought, water storage, and population growth prompted the Senate in August of 1886 to require a status report from the Department of Agriculture on irrigation and reclamation possibilities in the region. The assignment was handed to Richard Hinton. The veteran journalist had a broad knowledge of the West, vast experience in compiling and interpreting historical and statistical data, and he wrote in a clear, concise style. With a small staff to help him, Hinton immediately mailed a questionnaire to hundreds of people out west — engineers, irrigationists, land owners, arboriculturists, and colonists. Three months later, he had gathered sufficient information for a report on water conditions in the western states and territories.

On December 15, Hinton's 240-page survey, "Irrigation in the United States — Its Extent and Methods, with a digest of laws governing water supply," was transmitted to the Senate. The document focused on the region west of the 100th meridian, and touched on a multitude of subjects: rainfall and humidity, settlement, lumber and grass destruction, water sources and distribution, and irrigation projects. Most of the arid west was reclaimable, Hinton stated, but added that at least one-third of it had water problems. An appendix carried essays on irrigation developments in Mexico and Australia.

Hinton's report provided a detailed introduction to a problem of growing national interest, and placed him in the forefront of the crusade for government support for large-scale irrigation projects to open new lands to agriculture. Beginning in 1888, Congress appropriated funds for extensive irrigation surveys and created a Special Commitee on Irrigation and Reclamation of Arid Lands. One of the first actions of the Committee was to request Hinton to revise, expand, and update his 1886 report.

Colonel Hinton was appointed "Special Agent in Charge of Artesian Wells Investigation" in the spring of 1890. With broader responsibilities, he divided his inquiry into three parts, and set his thirteen member staff collecting data on engineering, geology, and state surveys. He also sought information on the best artesian well sites between the 97th meridian and the foothills of the Rockies. A 398-page study was ready by August 20. This report contained a number of detailed reports, several maps, and lengthy statistical tables concerning artesian well operation. But Congress wanted more — and quickly voted funds for a study "to determine the extent and availability for irrigation of the underflow and artesian waters" in the prairie belt stretching from Montana to Texas. Elevated to head the Office of Irrigation Inquiry, Hinton went west by train to coordinate field work. In early February of 1891, he filed a progress report based on correspondence and questionnaires, promising a more detailed study within a year.

The 1892 report was the capstone of Hinton's irrigation inquiries. He had personally visited the principal irrigation districts in twelve western states and obtained data on the status of reclamation in each. In many of the states, he said, there had been considerable legislative and judicial activity regarding water management, but more supervision of water resources was needed. Hinton took pride in the two experimental farms that his office had set up in South Dakota; in both cases the land was irrigated by water from artesian wells. Finally, for purposes of comparison, he appended general reports on irrigation developments in several foreign countries. With the submission of this voluminous document, Colonel Hinton completed his extended term of government service and returned again to full-time journalism.

Hinton's government work carried him into the mainstream of the irrigation crusade. The drought of 1890 had caused an outcry in the West for federal assistance, and William E. Smythe, editor of the *Omaha Bee,* had begun a campaign to arouse public support for large-scale projects in the Western states and territories. Smythe enlisted the support of Richard Hinton to write articles and give speeches. Hinton joined the crusade with enthusiasm. At the National Irrigation Congress in Los Angeles in 1893, he created somewhat of a scene by challenging Major John Wesley Powell, head of the Geological Survey, who spoke at the meeting. Hinton challenged the bureaucrat's warning that there was insufficient water for large reclamation projects, and called for legislation to develop the arid lands.

About this time, Hinton also published an article entitled "The Newer West" in *The Forum* magazine. In the article he forecasted a great future for the region west of the 98th meridian. In his recent travels on government business, he had visited eighteen Western states and territories. This area contained a population of 5 million — but it conceivably could support 100 million. "The new population of the newer West," Hinton wrote, was "the most marvelous of all its striking features." It seemed that "a draft had been made upon the Central States and the old North-west for their younger men and women." There was "nothing rustic or unusual either in their dress or ways." Pioneer life was passing; even the cowboy was fading from the scene. Only faint traces remained of the "crude life" of the mining camp, or of "the louder and coarser vulgarity and license of that carnival of vice and crime which so marked a feature of the 'railroad front.'" The shrill cry of "Keno" might still be heard in some mountain towns, but "in such centers of coarse masculinity" the echoes were growing feebler. Civilization was "assuming a show of virtue, 'even if it hath it not.'"

The "sublime physical features" of the Newer West would shape its development and destiny. The chief factor was aridity. Here, water had to be "artificially applied to the soil, otherwise fertile," if agriculture and horticulture were to be "in any wise successful pursuits." Livestock raising also was limited by the arid conditions. Another controlling factor was uncertain rainfall, which varied from mountains to plains, from tablelands to valleys and basins. To provide a predictable supply of water, large federal "storm and flood storage works" were needed. Hinton recognized the arguments of the "constitutional expounders" but asserted that the safety of the commonwealth required "the reassumption of its sovereignty" over western lands and rivers. Congress, or the Supreme Court, must lay down rules for interstate appropriations of water; drainage basins should take precedence over state boundaries. Public control of the western waters was essential.

Hinton predicted that the Newer West would acquire a commercial position of vast importance. The Pacific Ocean would become "the new world's Mediterranean," and provide a highway to the Orient, where nearly one half of the globe's inhabitants lived. The American shores of the Pacific must rapidly develop into a region of great "commercial progress and power." In time the Newer West might demand — and even absorb — the west coast of Canada and the peninsula of Lower California. The laws of physical unity demanded this. Hinton's article was reprinted as a pamphlet and widely distributed.

Richard Hinton capitalized on his government survey work in other ways. For example, he offered his services as a private "consulting irrigation expert." In 1893 he published a study he had made for the Valverde Land and Irrigation Company on the Armendaris Grant in New Mexico Territory. Hinton stated that he recently had interviewed residents on the grant, and inspected its topography, drainage, soils, and rainfall records. He listed four possibilities for irrigation on the grant: 1) building storage basins in canyons to catch the runoff; 2) drilling artesian wells (a well 160 feet deep near Engle was active); 3) opening canals from the Rio Grande; and 4) sinking shallow wells near the banks of rivers. Hinton went into great detail, and cited reports by a host of engineers and agricultural specialists. It was his view that nearly 300,000 acres in Socorro and Sierra counties could be open to cultivation if several of the projects could be built.

Hinton's interest in the Southwest extended into other fields besides irrigation. He wrote an article for *Frank Leslie's Popular Monthly* entitled "The Deserts of America." In this essay, he advanced theories about the formation of the deserts in Arizona, focusing particularly on the Papaguería (southwestern part of the territory) and the Yuma area. Even bolder was his venture into archaeology. *Harper's* Weekly published his "The Great House of Montezuma" in 1889, which discussed the ancient Casa Grande ruin and other pre-historic remains in the Gila, Salt and Verde valleys of Central Arizona. Scientists were beginning serious investigations there and Hinton joined those who were describing and attempting to interpret the findings. While many writers speculated about the origins of the ruins, Hinton merely sought to describe and classify them. He divided the remains into six categories: enclosures, cliff dwellings, great houses, mounds, excavations, and fortifications. Hinton's article provided the general reading public with an interesting introduction to pre-Columbian civilization of the Southwest.

In the mid-nineties, the veteran journalist settled in New York. He was almost deaf, but his spirit and energy was unflagging. Several memoirs on the John Brown era in Kansas had appeared, and Hinton decided to publish his own version of those eventful days. The product was unfortunate. At its publication his work was severely criticized for editorial liberties with quoted matter and historical inaccuracies. For a man who had enjoyed respect in government circles for accurate reporting, the book tarnished rather than enhanced his reputation. Hinton doubtless wanted to present his version of the Brown episode, but he probably had an even more practical motive for writing the book. He needed money (he repeatedly badgered the government to increase his military pension) and sought to capitalize on a popular issue. In 1898 Hinton published his last work — a book of poems written by his English-born friend Richard Realf, a compatriot in Kansas. In the summer of 1901, he sailed for "auld England" for a visit, and suffered a stroke and died there on December 20 at the age of seventy-one.

For over forty years, Richard Hinton had traveled and written about the West. In Kansas, on the Missouri border, in California and the Southwest, and finally on the prairie plains of the Newer West, he had viewed first-hand the growth and development of the nation's far-ranging hinterland. The West offered unlimited opportunities for the common man, and he believed that the representatives from that region would promote and expand these opportunities. Much of Hinton's writing focused on the Southwest, where he was somewhat of an anomaly, a man who identified with the land, yet had no roots in it. He found the area unique — and as a last frontier, it made good copy. Through his writings thousands of readers gained their initial knowledge and impressions of the region. A curious little man, generous to a fault, Richard Josiah Hinton helped provide both insight and dimension to a significant chapter in Southwestern history.

# J. ROSS BROWNE AND ARIZONA

Richard H. Dillon

❧⳾ℬ⳾

ONE CAN HARDLY DIAGNOSE J. Frank Dobie and Walter S. Campbell, alias Stanley Vestal, as bookmen suffering from literary myopia, for if any Westerners ever personified 20-20 bibliographical vision it was the Texan and the Oklahoman.

Yet neither man included J. Ross Browne's early volume of Arizona travel and description, *Adventures in the Apache Country,* in his personal selection of best Southwestern books although the volume is, increasingly, earning the title of a classic among students and collectors of Arizoniana. One might assume that Arizona Territory lay beyond their horizon; that the curvature of the earth was just too great for old *Pimería Alta* and *Apachería* to be discerned from viewpoints in Austin and Norman. Not exactly. Admittedly, Dobie and Vestal were weak on Arizona and cited such thin narratives (as Dobie himself confessed) as Dane Coolidge's *Arizona Cowboys* while overlooking Martha Summerhayes entirely. But neither Dobie or Vestal failed to notice a better-written book than Browne's, a true Arizona classic — Captain John G. Bourke's *On the Border With Crook.* As is the case with Browne, the writing skill of General George Crook's Boswell is still not appreciated enough. This is so although the soldier, an Irishman like Browne, was praised as an ethnologist by F. W. Hodge and elected president of the American Folklore Society. Bourke is strangely missing from Lawrence Clark Powell's *Southwest Classics.* But Dobie described his magnum opus as "a truly great book on both Apaches and Arizona frontier," while Vestal called it "a book the Southwest may be proud of."

Is the neglect of J. Ross Browne by Dobie and Vestal inexplicable? Was their joint sin of omission purely a fluke? A matter of double oversight? This is highly unlikely. Did they possibly downgrade the voluminous Browne as a hack because of his prolific literary output? We are probably nearer the truth here. Browne, like his friend and fellow traveler, Bayard Taylor, and unlike his friend and Arizona traveling companion, Charles Poston (and unlike Bourke, or Cremony, &c&c, for that matter), was not a soldier, not a miner, not merely a traveler. He was a professional, a working writer — with all the pluses and minuses of that lonely and unremunerative occupation.

Quick-witted and thoughtful, Browne was an addict of words and highly skilled in their use. He was humorous and insightful. He knew how to mix brevity with levity in order to create interest, and to make his style pungent with irony. As Carl Wheat observed in relation to Browne's *Crusoe's Island,* his writings "display the workings of a keen and critical mind."

But Browne was also harried and harassed by deadlines and hounded by bill collectors, like every other freelance in history since the first troglodyte chipped his first graffito at Lascaux. Poor distracted Browne was sometimes forced by circumstances to scatter his shots, to hurry his work; to aim for the timely, the topical, the popular when he might have addressed matters of more permanence. Often he was obliged to produce a prose product without time to polish it to the bright lustre it deserved. His Apache opus is typical of the Irish-American's writing while "under the gun." If *Adventures in the Apache Country* is an Arizona classic it is a flawed classic.

The book documents Browne's zealous "mining" of his material in order to beat off creditors. Critics — the well-fed sort, such as pedantic, tenured professors — resent this repetition, this recycling of literary material by authors who have rent to pay, a wife to house, children to feed — solely by the profits of the pen. Faced with yet another *lobo* at the door, Browne not only presented his Arizona observations to San Franciscans in a series of articles in the *Daily Evening Bulletin* from January through April of 1864, he then worked them up into lead articles for *Harper's New Monthly Magazine* for October 1864–March 1865, before combining the sketches into the first edition of *Adventures in the Apache Country* in 1869. And then he padded what, from the title, appeared to be an Arizona book by adding an equal number of pages on his Nevada adventures. By this device, he expanded the volume to salable bulk for the bookstores of the 1860s.

It is unfortunate that Browne did not simply ransack the jam-packed cupboard of his fertile imagination to beef up *Apache Country* with additional details of his stay in the Territory. Instead, he chose to tack on "Washoe Revisited," "Bodie Bluff," "The Walker River Country," "The Dead Sea of the West," and "The Reese River Country." The compressing of two disparate books into the compass of one volume was a mistake, and the non-Arizona half, in fact, has been deliberately peeled away and discarded in the latest reprint edition. This expurgation gives a prime Arizona document — "classic" or not — a coherence and focus which was always weakened by the extraneous material.

To be sure, others have made up for Browne's seeming neglect by Dobie in his *Guide to Literature of the Southwest* and Vestal's *The Book Lover's Southwest*. The late Charles Camp, for example, in the Wagner-Camp bible of Western Americana, *The Plains and the Rockies,* cited the six-part, eighty-page magazine serial antecendent of the book, "A Tour Through Arizona." Camp, no mean writer himself, not only referred to the inherent interest of Browne's articles and the fact that they were illustrated with clever woodcuts after the author's own sketches (for Browne was a talented and amusing artist), but stressed that it was a well-written narrative, too.

The late Francis Farquhar, while admitting that Browne's adventures had little to do with the Colorado River proper, found the book worthy of note in his bibliography, *The Books of the Colorado River and the Grand Canyon,* because of its description of Yuma and the Colorado Desert. But even more so because of a new element which the work brought to Western writing in the '60s. This was the Irishman's introduction of humor into Western travel literature. It would shortly be improved upon, indeed transformed into literature, by the genius of Mark Twain. As Larry Powell has mentioned in his writings, it was J. Ross Browne's misfortune to be a writer of talent preceding, in Twain, a man of genius. But Browne pioneered the *Roughing It* genre and made it a part of Western Americana for a truly national audience.

*Adventures in the Apache Country* has hardly been neglected by bibliographers. It will be found in Boyer, Bradford, Eberstadt, Edwards, Farquhar, Field, Graff/Storm, Heard/Hamm, Howes, Munk/Alliott, Rader, Streeter, Wagner-Camp and God knows what else. But to return to its neglect. One wonders if Dobie and Vestal were perplexed by the book in the same way the dean of Chicago bibliopoles, Wright Howes, was. He included Browne in his highly selective bibliography, *U.S.iana,* of 10,000 significant and uncommon titles though the book is hardly rare, even today. It must be one of the most common of "uncommon" books which Howes admitted to his "a" coding, meaning a book which could be found, *circa* 1962, in the out-of-print market place for a price between ten and twenty-five dollars.

For *Adventures in the Apache Country,* like the less well-written *Captivity of the Oatman Girls* by Royal B. Stratton, was a best-seller in its 1869, 1871, and 1878 American editions and its German (Jena) translation of 1871, *Reisen und Abenteuer im Apachenlande.* Howes allowed it into his bibliocorral solely because of its merit, not its scarcity. Were it not so worthy a book intrinsically, it would have fallen into Howes's enormous (and debatable) blanket-exclusion category of inexpensive, i.e., cheap or "common" books which he equated, cavalierly, with trivia, simply because of their low cash value in the modern out-of-print market.

As more reprints of *Apache Country* appear (one in 1950, two in 1974 alone, for example), the respect for Browne's book increases. The distinguished U.S.C. history professor and authority on Western Americana, Dr. Doyce B. Nunis, in a *Westways* book review page, rated it alongside *Vanished Arizona,* by Martha Summerhayes, as a volume which should be found in every bibliography on Arizona's territorial history. And while it it true that dustjacket copy and sales catalog blurbs must be viewed with suspicion, it would not appear that the University of Arizona Press was speaking with a forked tongue in its catalog of 1974 publications. It described the Tucson edition, edited by Donald Powell of the University Library, as "one of the best accounts of Southern Arizona in the Territorial days."

Don Powell's claim was echoed by John Espey in an August 1975 *Westways* book review column in which he extolled the dry reportorial style of Browne's thoroughly readable and basic book on pioneer Arizona, and saluted its welcome touches of irony.

The Eberstadt Americana catalogs perhaps sum up Browne's claim on regional literary immortality: "No other work gives so vivid or such an accurate account of the country, and the terrors which then attended border life in Arizona, where one-twentieth of the population had been swept away by the attacks of the Apaches in three years."

Wright Howes, like so many booksellers, collectors, librarians, professors and historians, was interested in factual Western Americana, books of a serious and fundamentally historical nature. Historical documentation was his cup of tea. Thus, he not only left out of his *U.S.iana* all scientific and technical works, but also books of history and travel if they were of an "imaginative nature," to use the Chicagoan's own words. Now, by this he meant fiction. And yet one wonders if Browne was not suspect because of the imaginative factor of creativity in his work. Perhaps this worked against his complete acceptance by Howes, Dobie and Vestal.

Browne — the most honest of civil servants, a veritable Diogenes of a Special Agent for the Government — most certainly did take liberties with facts in his writing. When it came to poetic license, J. Ross Browne must have held a low serial number. And yet his enlarging upon the facts was only cosmetic; he did not misstate the truth. And it is Browne's very imagination, humor, irony, creativeness — his literary skills — which make the book as readable today as Stratton's volume is not. J. Ross Browne never ceased to stumble over Spanish words, especially Hispanic place-names of the Southwest, but he is never guilty of the weepy sentimentality of Reverend Stratton's Victorian style.

What does Lawrence Clark Powell, the most broad-gauged of Southwest bibliographers, have to say about *Apache Country*? Plenty. Powell, like many of us who are not bibliographers (the latter, too often, resemble statisticians), is hooked on what the French call *la vice impunie*. This unpunished vice to which we shamelessly confess is *reading*. Browne is meant to be read, to be enjoyed, not just collected or listed or rated. He knew the English language intimately, and loved it; he played with it and, if he could not make it sing like some greater writers do, he made it hum!

Perhaps Browne is an acquired taste, like the olives of tradition or the *retsina* and *bacalhau* of reality. Certainly, Larry Powell started off slowly on him. In his *Southwestern Book Trails* of 1963, he lumped *Apache Country* with the interesting but less-important *Joseph Reddeford Walker and the Arizona Adventure* of Daniel Connors as worthwhile books to read. By 1974, with the publication of his excellent *Southwest Classics,* the scales had slithered off the Southern California emigré's eyes and J. Ross Browne of Oakland and points southeast took his place with the select company of ancients, like Kino, Garcés, Anza and Summerhayes in Arizona's literary Valhalla.

Powell realized that Browne's very popularity had worked against him after his death, just as has been the case with Bayard Taylor. Or, for that matter, with Robert Louis Stevenson, Jack London and John Steinbeck. Browne's tireless travel writing brought him the widest renown among literate Americans in the 1860s and 1870s. But he was speedily, and sadly, forgotten after his untimely death in 1875. His works have had to be kept alive by his aficionados, whose converts will, in turn, continue the task in the years ahead.

As Lawrence Clark Powell has also commented, Browne was not a man of genius. No Herodotus, no Plutarch, he was merely a man richly endowed with writing talent. He mixed history and biography, travel and description masterfully. He was a gifted craftsman. Personally, he was a real gentleman and that *rara avis,* an honest man. And he was a compulsive writer, as addicted as DeQuincey but to India ink and foolscap. Browne could no more swear off writing than he could give up breathing. He did not give a damn about his genius, would have whooped with laughter at *Apache Country* being termed a classic. Unworried about fame, either present or future, he had no time to waste in predicting how his personal literary lode would pan out, in time, in the assays of critics. He was like the hunter obsessed with the chase, not the kill or the trophy. Larry Powell noticed this in Browne and quoted him in *Southwest Classics*: "It is only the excitement of the action that governs me, I care nothing about the result."

Browne was the most devoted of husbands and fathers and cared more about his family than anything on earth, even his writing. He was hugely interested in seeing life, savoring it, but at the same time he was chained to duty, to the Victorian principle that he must never let his brood go hungry for a day as long as he could take up his pen. This utter dedication to his family, combined with financial insecurity and a bout of ill health, explain why his style in *Apache Country* is on a level with, say, that of John R. Bartlett (*Personal Narrative of Explorations*) rather that the graceful prose of John R. Bourke in *On the Border With Crook*. Browne simply did not have time to refine his prose, though he had the ability. He wrote in the field, with a tablet balanced on a dusty knee, and rushed his story to waiting printers in San Francisco and New York. Bourke, on the other hand, polished his recollections of the 1870s and 1880s until they shone like dragoons' brass buckles, and did not bring his Arizona reminiscences to print in *Century* magazine and in his book until 1891.

J. Ross Browne joined his old friend, Charles D. Poston, Lincoln's newly appointed Superintendent of Indian Affairs for Arizona, for an 1864 tour of Indian reservations and mining claims. (The new Supe was of a decidedly mineralogical, and speculative, bent.) Before he even reached Fort Yuma, Browne was in self-confessed "depressed spirits" because of sickness which made authorship difficult at best, and lively writing almost impossible. He was not only liverish, but suffering from diarrhoea. The latter, usually made light of as a nuisance, joked about as the "trots" or *turista* today, is a very debilitating complaint. And, like its opposite number, chronic constipation (which Robert Louis Stevenson deplored), it is destructive of literary creativity. Moreover, Browne was "worried sick" about his ability to keep up the mortgage payments on his Oakland home and to pay back the Government advance of $1,000 made to him while he was serving as Special Agent for the Bureau of Indian Affairs.

From Los Angeles, Browne wrote his wife on December 11, 1863, that it was a struggle for him to set forth on such a long trip while he was feeling so poorly. "But the hope of clearing off my debt to the Government and doing something for myself and family prompted me to hazard a great deal." He was afraid that Lucy might have to sell some of their lots in order to meet the most pressing demands for money. He even gave her permission to take his horse and buggy to San Francisco to sell at auction, should it become necessary. His worry over his family's straits was imprinted in every letter which he wrote home from Arizona. He vowed to do his best to make enough money in the Southwest to pay off all of his debts. Browne found it harder, this time, to leave his dear wife and children: "People who fancy I run off on these expeditions because I like it," he wrote Lucy, "do not know the effort it costs me. I believe my attachment to home — at least to my family — is the very strongest feeling in my nature."

David M. Goodman, in his biography of Browne, *A Western Panorama,* insists that the traveler had absolutely no connection with the Government while in Arizona. That is technically correct, but only technically so. He saw himself as still working for the Indian Bureau, with the connivance of Poston, to pay off the $1,000 advance. He wrote, ambiguously, in his book: "It was, incidentally, my business to look after the Indians, in virtue of an honorary roving commission from the Department of the Interior." He no longer held a Special Agent's commission, but this ambiguity was not finally cleared up until Lina Fergusson Browne published her *J. Ross Browne: His Letters, Journals and Writings* in 1969. She printed a letter he wrote to his wife from Fort Yuma on December 27, 1863, which sets the record straight. Not only was he paid as a consultant by Poston for his mining expertise, as they examined Arizona mines for possible development, he was the Superintendent's paid amanuensis. He wrote: "I have been busy all day writing my report to the Indian Bureau. I have worked very hard to get the accounts of the Superintendent in proper shape for transmission to the Department, and enjoy the satisfaction of knowing that I am gradually getting out of debt."

Browne was under the weather for almost the entire journey from Fort Yuma to the Pima Villages. He would have turned back except that he hated to give up in anything once he had decided to undertake it. He was in better physical and mental health by the time he reached Tucson, for all of the fatigues and dangers of Apache Land. There Poston offered him $5,000 in drafts on greenbacks, worth about $3,500 in gold when discounted, for his continued services. And he threw in some mining stock, to boot. Much cheered, Browne told his wife that with royalties from *Harper's* he might clear $10,000 from his Arizona adventure. He was hearty again and had added ten pounds as well as a full beard and a sun tan. He told Lucy on January 16, 1874: "You would scarcely know me, my health has improved so much." For the first time in his life, he actually grew fat. It did not last, however; like a jackrabbit (as he said), he lost it all again in about three day's time.

In California, Oregon and Washington, Browne had already proved himself to be a compassionate friend of the Indians. But he drew the line at the Apaches. He hated these raiders whom John C. Cremony, recalling India's criminal society, called "the Thugs of American aborigines." Though he was accompanied by an escort of troopers from General Carleton's California Column, Browne was uneasy, fearful, in Apachería. While he was in Arizona, Indians were murdering mining friends of Poston's and, like most Arizonans, Browne blamed the Oatman Massacre on the Apaches though it was actually the dirty work of the Yavapais.

Browne despised the Apaches because of their hit-and-run, skulking style of guerrilla warfare. He thought that it was not cricket, even for savages, and mistakenly confused their choice of tactics with cowardice. He wrote his wife: "They are great cowards, and will not fight if they can accomplish their objective by assassination."

The Apaches made Browne nervous. He feared for his scalp — and for his family, if left without him. It was an edgy author who wrote in *Apache Country*: "I never before traveled through a country in which I was compelled to pursue the fine arts with a revolver strapped around my body, a double-barreled shotgun lying across my knees, and half a dozen soldiers, armed with Sharps carbines, keeping guard in the distance."

From Yuma Crossing, Browne and Poston and their party followed the Gila River to Oatman Flat. Browne's matter-of-fact reporting of Olive Oatman's captivity, of which he had heard details from Henry Grinnell at Fort Yuma, was concise, dramatic, reporting. It is in refreshing contrast to the dated and tiring purplish prose of Reverend Stratton in his book on Arizona's epic tragedy, Arizona's equivalent of the Donner Party story in California lore. (R. B. Stratton. *The Captivity of the Oatman Girls*. New York, 1858).

Stratton, putting words in the lad's mouth, had Lorenzo describe Royse Oatman's sudden premonition of death in this fashion: "My father suddenly sank down upon a stone near the wagon and exclaimed, 'Mother, Mother, in the name of God, I know that something dreadful is about to happen!' In reply, our dear mother had no expressions but those of calm, patient trust, and a vigorous, resolute purpose . . ." (Followed by a burst of sentimental verse.)

Browne, in contrast, was content with a single, brief, summing-up sentence: "Hitherto, Mr. Oatman, naturally a man of sanguine temperament, had borne every disaster and braved every danger cheerfully and without flinching, but the presentiment of some terrible doom seemed to have fallen upon him at this place, and he was seen by some of the family to shed tears while sitting in the wagon."

Some of Browne's grimmest sketching of his entire career occurred on the Gila leg of his journey, between Oatman Flat and the Pima Villages. The first was a drawing of a dessicated, coyote-gnawed carcass of an Apache warrior hung on a tree, as a warning to others of his ilk, by frontiersman King Woolsey. The second was an even more chilling sketch of another dead Apache, this one actually crucified by the (non-Christian) Maricopas as a deterrent to their Apache enemies. The corpses of the hated Apaches left the usually compassionate, but already hardened, Browne almost unmoved. Of the first one, he said only that he gazed at it with strange feelings, otherwise unexplained. Of the second, he merely said that: "It was a strange and ghastly sight."

After a visit with the Pimas, and junkets to Casa Grande and Picacho, Browne reached Tucson. He found it a filthy place overrun with the sweepings of humanity, including Californians run out of San Francisco by the Vigilance Committee. San Xavier del Bac, on the other hand, was an unexpectedly pleasant surprise. But Tubac, the grand old presidial pueblo of Anza, was a deserted ruin, abandoned to Apache depredations like Santa Cruz and virtually all of the mines and ranches of southern Arizona.

Back at San Xavier, Browne received a letter from Lucy which gave his improving spirits a setback and cut short his Arizona adventure. She was ill and he was doubly troubled, fearing that the worry which he had expressed in early letters home might have affected her health. So, just when Browne was getting his desert legs and ready to tackle highland Arizona with pen and ink, he had to abandon his travels. He let Poston proceed to northern Arizona without him though he had written to Indian Commissioner William P. Dole of his great interest in the "Moquis" (Hopis), saying that they were "the most interesting, perhaps, of all the Indian races of this continent." He was destined never to see Cañón de Chelly, the Hopi mesas, or the Grand Canyon.

Naturally, *Harper's New Monthly,* with considerable vested interest, applauded his book and the "dashes of general humor which enliven it." But the book had a good press in general. *The Galaxy* approved of the "light, entertaining and abundantly illustrated book," while *Godey's Lady's Book* pronounced Browne's humor to be "laugh-provoking, adventurous, irrepressible." Period humor alone would not have saved Browne any more than it rescued Petroleum V. Nasby from oblivion. But H. H. Bancroft saw beneath the levity and praised Browne's book as unrivalled in terms of both interest and accuracy. Thomas Warren Field, in *An Essay Towards an Indian Bibliography* (1873) also made the point that Browne's entertaining account was a serious book. He stated: "Notwithstanding the air of mocking raillery with which the author envelopes most of the scenes he describes, his work has one great value, as it is a truthful portraiture of the terrors which attend border life in Arizona."

If he was not writing prose poetry, at least J. Ross Browne was composing a crisp, first-rate narration by the time he was forced to leave the Southwest for home. Typical was his last-page *adiós* to Arizona in *Adventures in the Apache Country*.

"No country that I have yet visited presents so many striking anomalies as Arizona. With millions of acres of the finest arable lands, there was not at the time of our visit a single farm under cultivation in the Territory; with the richest gold and silver mines, paper money is the common currency; with forts innumerable, there is scarcely any protection to life and property; with extensive pastures, there is little or no stock; with the finest natural roads, traveling is beset with difficulties; with rivers through every valley, a stranger may die of thirst. Hay is cut with a hoe and wood with a spade or mattock. In January one enjoys the luxury of a bath as under a tropical sun, and sleeps under double blankets at night. There are towns without inhabitants, and deserts extensively populated; vegetation where there is no soil, and soil where there is no vegetation. Snow is seen where it is never seen to fall, and ice forms where it never snows.

"There are Indians the most docile in North America, yet travelers are murdered daily by Indians the most barbarous on earth. The Mexicans have driven the Papagos from their southern homes and now seek protection from the Apaches in the Papago villages. Fifteen hundred Apache warriors, the most cowardly of the Indian tribes of Arizona, beaten in every fight with the Pimas, Maricopas and Papagos, keep these and all other Indians closed up as in a corral; and the same Apaches have desolated a country (Sonora) inhabited by 120,000 Mexicans. Mines without miners and forts without soldiers are common. Politicians without policy, traders without trade, storekeepers without stores, teamsters without teams, and all without means, form the mass of the white population. But here let me end, for I find myself verging on the Proverbs."

# REFLECTIONS ON
# THE POWELL-HARRISON CORRESPONDENCE
### Jake Zeitlin

❖❖❖

THE EDITORS OF THIS VOLUME laid down the condition that my contribution was not to be in the nature of a personal tribute to Larry Powell. What they specified was that it should be of the nature of an account of Southwestern life or letters, perhaps something dealing with the history of bookselling. Mrs. Kathleen Dakin Thompson has been for some months engaged in organizing the files of my bookselling history which have been deposited in the Special Collections Department of the University of California at Los Angeles. She has uncovered a number of illuminating and somewhat startling documents which I had reposed in my archives for almost forty years. But none of them have surprised or delighted me more than the records of a correspondence carried on under my very nose and without my knowledge between one of my most trusted employees and his friend Elston Harrison. If I had known how talented at evangelising, persuading and coercing that mild mannered young man was, I might have raised his salary and thereby might have deterred him from his subsequent career of distinction in the world of librarianship. I cannot help wishing that I could have discovered these letters while they were being written. What a great bookseller — or possibly con artist — Lawrence Clark Powell would have made.

It is my thesis that these letters uniquely illuminate life and letters in the Southwest and that they are therefore appropriate for inclusion in this volume. In addition, I offer them as evidence of that peculiar combination of wit, charm and rascality that makes Larry Powell the object of such an immense and constant torrent of affection, none greater than my own.

*Lawrence Clark Powell – Elston Harrison Correspondence*

The correspondence began on a formal note (March 30, 1935) "Dear Mr. Harrison . . ." and progressed to a less formal basis (July 23, 1935) "Dear Larry . . . Will write you in a couple of weeks . . . In the meantime — stay sober (moderately) . . ." (October 30, 1935, Powell to Harrison) ". . . . Had lunch with Jack S—— this noon. We took your name in vain — but not without some mild profanity . . ."

*January 4, 1936, Harrison to Powell:*

. . . Kansas is a dry state. You may have heard that. I haven't had a drink of any sort of liquor for six weeks . . .

Lately I have been reading a book which I bought from you mugs entitled "We are Betrayed" by Vardis Fisher. It would appear that I have been betrayed also. Numerous pages are mssing from the damn book. The paper is there all right but there are no printed words on it. What does a person do in a case like this? I am not sufficiently imaginative to finish the story on my own power and should prefer Mr. Fisher's version . . .

*January 10, Powell to Harrison:*

. . . Just too damn bad about the Vardis Fisher WE ARE BETRAYED; but I guess you might as well bring it along, and I'll type in the missing pps. of text. Please don't in the meantime feel in the least betrayed. If necessary I'll send the cursed book to Mister Fisher and have him fill out the blanks in longhand . . .

How about that Hemingway bullfighting book I wrote you about, you hound. I've had it put aside for you. Let me know or I'll sell it for double wot I asked . . .

P.S. Why *Topeka?* . . . [Harrison had moved to Topeka, Kansas]

*January 21, Powell to Harrison:*

I believe you have a first of John Steinbeck's TORTILLA FLAT. His new book, IN DUBIOUS BATTLE, will be out in a week or so. I am reserving a first for you. I think him our greatest California novelist; it is certain that his first editions are increasingly sought after. We have a mint copy in dust-wrapper of his third book, TO A GOD UNKNOWN, 1933, for $4.75. This is a sort of Jeffers in prose; it's laid in a valley back of the Big Sur. His second book, THE PASTURES OF HEAVEN, fetches $5.00; I have a mint copy of it also. His first book, THE CUP OF GOLD, is damned hard to find. In all my searching for his firsts during the past three months, I have turned up but one copy of this; and it was sold immediately on a special order. You can't go wrong on Steinbeck. I'll put the above mentioned two on reserve until I hear from you.

Just got in a nice first, sans dust-wrapper, of Hemingway's WINNER TAKE NOTHING, 1933. In case you don't have this, $2.50 will take it off the shelf.

And still I want to know, WHY TOPEKA?

*January 25, Harrison to Powell:*

No, you viper, I have a copy of *Winner Take Nothing,* and what is more I am not ordering any more books from your thieves' den until you replace at no extra cost my copy of *We Are Betrayed* with a copy that is complete and readable, the sort of a copy that a really high-class bookstore would sell me. You may consider this an indictment of your entire ideology.

And again — must I say? — Topeka, Topeka, well, why not Topeka?

*February 6, Harrison to Powell:*

. . . am returning the copy of *We Are Betrayed* which suffered from malnutrition. Hope you can get me a copy that is not sick. . . .

*March 2, Powell to Harrison:*

Yesterday was Sunday. I felt a bit low from a slight thrust of flu and so was draped along the couch thumbing a volume of the Encyclopedia Britannica. The volume in hand had a lot of K material in it. I read about Keats, and turning back found a lot about Kansas. So Topeka is the capital. Well, the point is, while reading about the elevation, the topography, the economics, etc., of Kansas, I thought of you . . .

Too bad you can't handle the Joyce at present. You ask about the Hemingway. I'm afraid — unless you make a killing — it will be too high. The price is around $90. His first book, THREE STORIES & TEN POEMS, printed in Dijon in 1923, by the same printer, by the way, who did Joyce's Ulysses (and Powell's Robinson Jeffers!). Auction records show it as high as $200. The copy I have in mind was bought by a chap in Paris when it came out. It's been in his possession ever since, and is a fine copy. I haven't seen it, but if you are tempted, let me know and I'll push a deal through. Frankly, I believe the Joyce at $75 very much the best bargain . . .

Starting this month I'm released from all clerical duties around the shop, and am now a 100% super salesman. Boy, look out for me! . . .

*April 7, Powell to Harrison:*

. . . Very glad to have word from you. I'd begun to think of you as a mysterious person, perhaps gone on a secret mission to Bessarabia or points east. Thanks a lot for the orders. The three knaughty books [*Fanny Hill, etc.*] have salted away in the little cache I'm holding for you . . . I have picked up two more real items in the line of contraband goods [Frank Harris, Richard Burton] . . . Here is a veritable mine of Oriental erotic tales and love, or should I say tails. It would be a stunning addition to the good books you already have and would provide stimulating reading on the many and many a cold night for years to come . . .

Not such long silence, please.

*April 27, Powell to Harrison:*

You're an awful bum to be having the flu. Why don't you come back to God's Country, grow a beard and be a real he-man? . . .

Have put the Russian book aside and absorbed the tax in the price as you chiseled me into doing on such items. A pox on you, scurvy rogue . . .

Am going to write you a really high pressured letter in a day or so. So be on your guard. . . .

*April 27, Powell to Harrison:*

The items I wanted to write you about came in sooner than I expected so here goes a second letter in the same day. I told you we have a fine copy of Robinson Jeffers' first book, FLAGONS & APPLES, in crimson morocco folding slip-case, at $40. We now have the finest copy I have ever seen of his second book, CALIFORNIANS (1916), absolutely perfect and a review copy to boot, with perforated title-page "Advance Copy, for review, Not for Sale." The price of this is $20. And thirdly, a first edition in dust-wrapper of ROAN STALLION, TAMAR & OTHER POEMS (1925) at $10. Here are three key books for a Jeffers collection. I'd like to see you get them. And here's how I propose to deal:

The total as above is $70. First we take $5 off the *Flagons,* then $5 off the *Californians,* then $2.50 off the *Roan Stallion.* Then what do we have? A total of $57.50 — that holds if you take the three. And believe me, these three books can't be bought for anywhere near as low anywhere else, exclamation point. As an added inducement (as if you needed any) I will ship the three to Robinson Jeffers at Tor House and have them inscribed to you, as we did the *Apology for Bad Dreams*. Thus you will have presentation copies of all three items, and at a lower cost than you paid for the single *Apology for Bad Dreams*. I think it a grand bargain.

Let me know by return air-mail/ I really believe you can't afford to pass this up. . . .

*April 28, Harrison to Powell:*

I had hoped that my last letter to you would hush you up for all time but you are the most persistent nuisance I have ever encountered. You should be in the oil business. You fairly reek with the spirit of Los Angeles. Egad!

Relative to the three Jeffers items my offer is $50.00 *net cash,* said $50.00 (cash) to be forthcoming from me *immediately* upon notification from you of the acceptance of this offer. All three items are to be inscribed to me by Dr. Jeffers and not by yourself. There is a similiarity between Jeffer's writing and yours, nor would it surprise me greatly for you to palm off such a stunt on me.

And that's that.

*May 1, Harrison to Powell:*

I take great pleasure in penning the enclosed check. It makes me realize fully that I am the world's greatest sucker — and in being that there is both quality and merit.

I didn't want the damn books, I shall probably never read them and I know that I am paying an amount in excess of their value on the market by at least twice. I blame my undoing on your insidious personality. I have been worked on by experts but you are the tops.

What became of the guy who had $70.00 in gold for the damn things? The reason I ask is that I wonder if you ever hear strange voices calling you or if you see things under your bed.

I detest petty liars but admire sincere frauds.

Please don't congratulate me or tell me how lucky I am when I've made a thorough ass of myself . . .

I hope you have no illusions about the people you mention "who are clamoring right this moment at the front door." They are not ululating for Jeffers' books, but for your hide.

Permit me to admonish you to be more circumspect in your actions henceforth. In San Francisco years ago a group of outraged citizens organized a judiciary body known as the "vigilantes" whose function it was to eradicate persons and parties given to nefarious practices. I see by the liberal weeklies that there has been a recent recrudescence of this historic group in various sections of California. Hence I am fearing for your safety. . . .

*May 4, Powell to Harrison:*

Thanks for the check. It came just as the sheriff's men were forcing the front door. Now we are once more wide open. Caveat emptor.

Your low and abusive letter has come to my attention. Nothing however deters me. I am firm in my resolve to see you get nothing but the finest and most expen I mean cheapest books — and lots of em every month, you wolf in oilskins . . .

Yes, I was going to ship you the three Jeffers books when they came back from Carmel. Don't want them around because I'd be tempted to sell them again to someone else. However in the face of your pleadings, I'll sock them away for you, along with the rest of the junk I mean priceless rarities you've bought from me . . .

I believe you have firsts of the Vardis Fisher tetralogy. Now how about his first two novels, Toilers of the Hills and Dark Bridwell? Can get you a mint 1st of the latter for $3.50 — am still angling for the former.

Now listen, you Kansas cyclone, you need a copy of Hemingway's first publication THREE STORIES & TEN POEMS, Dijon, 1923. Scarcer than pedestrains on Wilshire Boulevard. Give me confirmation that you are determined to have this at a reasonable price and I think I can pull one out of somebody's sleeve. Also believe I can still get the first in original blue wrappers of James Joyce ULYSSES (Dijon 1922) for $75. Better not pass it up. Let me know. Don't get out of the buying mood. Any let down on your part will lead to firmer measures on my part. Mille regards. JAKE ZEITLIN INK.!

*May 11, Powell to Harrison:*

. . . Crawl out of the pipe-line and let me have another of your unusually complimentary epistles.

With hearty curses, . . .

Harrison obliged:

*May 13, Harrison to Powell:*

Obstinate and Incorrigible Oaf —
I had hoped to be rid of you for all time but I see that you are impervious to hint, advice or suggestion . . .

You now offer me $3.50 *Dark Bridwell*. I am pleased to accept this offer as I know that the $2.50 profit that the sale affords you now and the pleasure that you derive from same will be more than compensated on some near tomorrow by a feeling on your part of the deepest, bitterest *remorse*. That is my sole reason for buying the book.

When you discover *Toilers of the Hills* please do not arrogate unto yourself the airs of a Jason returning home with the Golden Fleece. There are copies of this book (mint condition) in every other bookstore in Los Angeles and these copies are sold at about 50¢ @. I await with a certain degree of tension your "discovery" of the volume, not that there is any merit in the book itself, but there is merit in the Olympian fabrications which you weave around the discovery of a dime novel, just as there is a certain merit in a Gargantua taking a crap . . .

My sermon for the day concludes.

Cordially hating you, I remain

Your sincerest enemy,

Elston. . . .

*May 15, Powell to Harrison:*

In the 24 hours which have passed, since I last wrote you, history has been made. I have unearthed the most extraordinary, rare and ephemeral Robinson Jeffers item that it has ever been my privilege to handle. It is the Robinson Jeffers Supplement to The Carmelite, his hometown newspaper, published way back in the dim golden days of 1928. Very few copies were printed, and certainly most of these have gone the way of all small-town literature, aye, the way of all flesh: down the hatch to lethe. No copy has ever been sold at auction, and to the best of my considerable (!) knowledge, none has ever been catalogued or sold by a bookshop. Rarity, thy name is this Jeffers Supplement.

By dint of extraordinary powers of snooping, finegling and consumating, I have come into the possession of this superlatively rare sheet, and I am herewith offering you, basest of all rascals, the first crack at it. Any price which might be set would of course be arbitrary. Jake says one hundred dollars. Others say even higher. I however knowing the extreme meagerness of your present book budget and that mean streak in you which demands bargain prices on even the costliest and rarest of items, am setting the price at $25.00 — no more, no less — for a cash deal.

This will undoubtedly be the most prized item in your already valuable Jeffers collection — and you will take unmeasured pride in knowing that yours is one of the few copies in existence. I am the only person I know of who has another copy; mine was given me by Jeffers when I was there in 1933, and is inscribed by him, as well as by Lincoln Steffens and Ella Winter. Doubtless I could persuade him to do likewise with yours.

As you may well imagine, I have pleasant relations with numerous Jeffers collectors, here and in many foreign lands, and I have hardly to raise a finger to dispose of such a frail and desirable item. I can hardly understand my own magnanimous impulse which permits me to offer this to you, prior to all others, at a price which is tantamount to giving the thing away. I think I had better halt this generous letter before my cold reason gets the better of me and crosses out all that precedes this.

Yr. humble & obed. servt. . . .

P.S. Listenyourat, here's a description of the damned thing. See that you read it carefully.

*May 20, Harrison to Powell:*

Have been very busy in the last couple of days moving. Please note new address . . .

Your terrific sales talk regarding the new Jeffers item overwhelms me and I am inclined to bite. If it is still available please have it inscribed and put away with the rest of the junk. Am enclosing check . . .

P.S. This is written in such a hurry that I have no time to tell you what I really think of you, you scoundrel! . . .

*May 22, Powell to Harrison:*

You are a lucky devil. Imagine getting The Jeffers Carmelite for $25.00. Can such things be? And thanks for the check!

Moved again, eh? Why don't you try paying rent.

Now let's talk turkey. On March 3rd I wrote you about Hemingway's first book, THREE STORIES AND TEN POEMS, Dijon, 1923, and that I thought I could get you a copy for about $90.00. Ever since that time I have been negotiating for the copy in question, trying to effect a saving which I in turn could pass on to you . . . And now today I can report that by superhuman effort I have closed the deal. The book is ours and what a beauty it is! Best of all, the price is down, way down, to wit, $75.00. Simply unheard of. Unprecedented. Only one copy was sold at auction last year, a fair one, and it brought $110.00. Remember, auction prices are wholesale prices. That means that some dealer paid one hundred and ten for the item, and probably resold it for nearer two hundred. I have advertised extensively for the book. I am enclosing the last offer I got, of several months ago. The wholesale price to us of $200 gives you an indication of the extreme scarcity and desirability of the item.

Three hundred copies of THREE STORIES & TEN POEMS were printed in the summer of 1933 by Maurice Darantière in Dijon. The year before the same gentleman printed Joyce's ULYSSES. Our copy is in the original blue gray wrappers, entirely uncut. It is a very fine copy, with only a few faint smudges on the wrapper which can be cleaned up easily. The original owner in whose hands it has been since he bought it in Paris when issued has written his name on the fly-leaf — he is a noted American artist and this ads to the interest of the copy.

I am really quite excited over this book. It is the first one I have ever been able to get hold of, and it will be with great reluctance that I will part with it.

If we had to buy this book from another dealer the price would be at least twice as much. It is only on rare occasions such as this when we can get valuable books direct from the owners that we can scoop the market and turn them over at ridiculously low prices.

If you decide to get this succulent item — and I don't see how you can possibly afford to pass it up — you should have a protective case made for it. I could negotiate such for you at cost — about $2.00. And you really should have the same for "Californians," and a cloth portfolio for The Carmelite. "Flagons & Apples" is already boxed.

I am holding the Hemingway in our vault, and until I hear from you, I will not breathe a word of it to anyone. Jake is champing at the bit, but I believe I can hold him off for a few days longer. . . .

*June 2, Harrison to Powell:*

Since Bunk is apparently the most dominant characteristic of your personality and its verbal expression the most suitable means of communicating with you, I take pen in hand to set forth in terms of Bunk what's so and what isn't.

The Hemingway item is not a perfect copy by any means. It has someone's name written in it and that cuts down its value something terrific. The price of $75.00 may or may not be a fair price; I do not know. I doubt if anything in excess of $75.00 would be fair and I doubt if you could get any more than that, etc., etc., etc. I would like to own the item. . . . It is my suggestion that you let me have the book at $75 and I shall pay you $10 a month for six months and $15.00 the seventh month. This is the way I bought my car. (The car turned out to be an awful lemon, too.) Anyhow, there's the deal as far as I'm concerned.

*June 2, Powell to Harrison:*

... Regarding the Hemingway "Three Stories and Ten Poems" which I have on reserve for you, I hope you will let me have word pronto. Both Jake and Miss Manning have customers for this exquisite rarity, and it's a pushover at 75 bucks. Off the dime, you horses caboose, or I'll send it to you C.O/D just to get rid of it ...

[A] ... choice manuscript ... which we have here now is that of Liam O'Flaherty's THE RETURN OF THE BRUTE. There are 9 separate manuscript versions of the beginning, ranging from three lines to eight pages, under the provisional titles of "Revolt" and "The Murder of Corporal Williams", with two odd pages of manuscript of the same book; in all 27 pages of manuscript. In addition, there is the typescript of the major portion of the book (covering the first nine chapters and lacking only the last twenty pages) differing considerably from the published version (naughty words later deleted by publishers); in all 81 pages with six odd pages of typescript. With a few corrections and alterations in the author's hand.

It is interesting to see the genesis of the story, and it is infrequent that so many drafts of a story are ever preserved. O'Flaherty is certainly the outstanding young Irish pen-wielder, and since the success of "The Informer" he is hotter than ever. We want 100 bucks for the lot.

Now just to suck up whatever chicken-feed you have left, there is the limited edition of D. H. Lawrence's Letters at 15 dollars, mint in box ...

A fine copy — oh hell, let's call it a day.

Pen in pot, prince, and let's see what new blasphemy you can concoct. Regards and maledictions. ...

*June 5, Powell to Harrison:*

I'm glad to hear you want the Hemingway. I have charged it to your account, wrapped it snugly and put it out in the alley with the rest of your nuggets. Your scheme of financing gives me a pain in the neck. Six months my eye. I'll give you three. In the meantime, I suggest you slip us a check in response to the recent statement sent you. I'd like to get the decks clear so that I can unload something really big on you. ...

Powell eventually decided to leave bookselling and attend library school at the University of California at Berkeley. He wrote a final letter to Harrison:

*July 20, 1936:*

Just back from hunting a house in Berkeley to find your semi-scurrilous letter redeemed only by the check for 100 bucks. Many thanks. No more will I dun you, and I'm leaving instructions here for the others not to bother you too much. Your book wants will be well taken care of if you address them to Bessie Manning . . . Bessie has been here a year and knows her stuff . . .

Elston you rat, in spite of your surly chiseling disposition I have enjoyed fleecing you. Don't be surprised if I sell you the Golden Gate Bridge. My address is 2726 Derby Street, Berkeley. We are going up in about a week and will be there nearly a year. Let me hear from you; you'll hear from me.

So long!

# THE MAKING OF A NOVEL:
## THE SEARCH FOR THE DEFINITIVE TEXT
## OF D. H. LAWRENCE'S
## "THE PLUMED SERPENT"

L. D. Clark

✣❦✣

THE HISTORY OF THE CONCEPTION, composition and publication of *The Plumed Serpent* involves not only an interesting look into the author's ways of writing, but also reflects in an especially illuminating fashion the deeper currents of his mind and art during a crucial period of his life. Almost from the time America loomed as a hope in his future, Lawrence no doubt contemplated writing about it. This was during the early days of the first World War, when escape from what he conceived of as a dying England to some virgin land seemed imperative. The flight was not to be accomplished, at this time, except through the imagination. In the later stages of the war, Lawrence first began the actual process of creating an America for himself, a long while before he had ever seen the continent with his own eyes. These earliest attempts were not fiction; they were essays on classic American authors like Cooper and Melville, essays which Lawrence at first prepared to write, or to give as lectures, in America. To these prose endeavors to comprehend America from a distance may be added a few significant poems, written before Lawrence's sailing to America when the pull in that direction was particularly strong. The America visible in all these writings, fiction or not, is nonetheless a "creation" of Lawrence's own, revolving upon human character. At the core of all of them is the same concern as that of the actual fiction later on: how the transplanted European spirit, through a process of death and resurrection, may find accord with the spirit of American place and press forward toward a new flowering of mankind. The process of writing *The Plumed Serpent* was complex because his sense of America's place grew as he wrote.

For some three-and-a-half years after the Great War, Lawrence off and on weighed going to America, and more than once expressed his fascination with the Southwest and with Mexico. He received a letter from Mabel Dodge inviting him to come and live in her "colony" in Taos and write about the Indians, just as he was in one of his strongest moods to see America, in the autumn of 1921. He was soon making plans to go, and to do a kind of travel book on the States similar to his *Sea and Sardinia,* which was just about to appear in print. He did not speak of fiction set in America, however, until he was almost on the final leg of the round-the-world voyage by which he at last arrived in New Mexico about a year after the initial invitation. This voyage was a sort of psychological preparation to confronting the idea of fiction about America. That far-ranging resistance-attraction by which Lawrence responded to the magnetism of the new continent would not permit him to go straight to his goal across the Atlantic. Melville and Dana had put into his head the remote Pacific as a natural pathway to the strangeness of America. He therefore began a journey from Sicily which carried him briefly to Ceylon, and then, for something over three months, to Australia. It was truly Australia, the farthest of all continents to a European, together with the Pacific, which granted Lawrence the time of dormancy and expectation so essential to his approach toward America.

As soon as he was settled in a cottage on the ocean front south of Sydney, Lawrence began a novel set in Australia, *Kangaroo.* He wrote Mabel Dodge to say that he would remain here until the novel was finished, indicating also, in the clearest possible way, that his present actions were in his own mind a preliminary to whatever he might create in America: "I build quite a lot on Taos — and the pueblo. I shall be so glad if I can write an American novel from that centre. It's what I want to do. And I have learned a lot coming here."[1] In other words, the prepartion for the seed of what was to become *The Plumed Serpent* originated in Lawrence's decision to write *Kangaroo,* and to linger in Australia as if on a threshold.

What Lawrence had learned in Australia was simply to face what America was in the psychic projection of his feelings. How complex this projection was is evident from the elaborateness of his approach to the new land. Fundamentally, America represented to Lawrence the remotest reaches of time and place identical with that region in the human soul where the dark gods of blood-consciousness still held sway, the only gods through whom human harmony with the cosmos might be restored. But this religious impulse in Lawrence was generated out of a dual nature, a male and a female side of him, both deeply identified with America and often at cross purposes with one another. In the American fiction he finally wrote, all the questing protagonists come from far off in search of regeneration on the western continent. They are all women, and all are clearly to some extent surrogates of himself. The soul in the form of a woman in rebellion against modern life desires to be overcome and swept away by the noble, wild and powerful genius of primitive America. But the complementary action in the process springs from a being made also in Lawrence's own image. He desired to see himself embodied in the form of the primeval male, who in the magnificence of blood-knowledge will lead these pilgrim women on into the age to come. Thus atunement with America meant to him the achievement of a true male identity.

In *Kangaroo* both the male and female forces are already strongly active. The bulk of the novel concentrates on the problems of male identity, of loyalty and love between males, of male leadership by blood authority most of all. It is a great season of trial for the pilgrim Richard Somers, Lawrence's obvious fictional self. He must slough off all the old mistaken combinations of blood loyalty and political loyalty, including, as a culmination of these, an incarnation composed largely of the Australian spirit of place itself, the man Kangaroo. Kangaroo unfortunately contains as the other principal spirit of his make-up that old mental-spiritual abomination, to Lawrence and Somers, of charity, of love, which long ago usurped the place of the dark gods and started man on his disastrous course. At the end of the novel, Somers is more or less free and ready to pursue his way toward the meeting with the dark gods over the great waters in America. And his wife, Harriet, also with considerable author identification, comes forward in the last chapter, which was rewritten in New Mexico. She prepares the way for the delineation of Lawrence's American heroines. Something like the bird-and-reptile dichotomy of Kate Leslie's struggle in *The Plumed Serpent* is already present in Harriet Somers. The freedom that Australia first gave her has turned sour, freedom in itself being nothing, and she is ready to accept her husband's preaching that you cannot escape "the dark hand of the Lord"[2] leading you on to submission to the proper gods.

According to Mabel Dodge, Lawrence had scarcely arrived in Taos, in September, 1922, when he undertook to put into effect his hopes of writing an American novel. But this was not to prove at all easy. The material to create a fictional surface was readily at hand, for Mabel Dodge's experiences appeared exactly fitted to Lawrence's demands for a subject. She had repudiated her three previous marriages and presumably the world of modern civilization with them. She had come west in search of a new life. She now had an Indian lover and what at least in a novel might be treated as the motivation to establish contact with the lost dark gods. Indeed, Lawrence departed little from the basic pattern of Mabel Dodge's life to produce heroines in any of his American fiction. This was not because she herself represented an irresistible inspiration, but simply because her life was so much a case in point in Lawrence's view of modern dilemmas.

The actual novel based on her experiences never got beyond a scene or two and some notes, but we know from these that the heroine was to arrive in New Mexico on her quest, was to meet in Santa Fe the husband with whom she was at odds, was to drive on to Taos under the influence of feelings no doubt analogous to those which Lawrence had enjoyed on first seeing northern New Mexico and which he expressed years later in this way: "The moment I saw the brilliant, proud morning shine high up over the deserts of Santa Fe, something stood still in my soul, and I started to attend.[3] Once arrived in Taos, the heroine was soon to be intimately involved with the Indian lover. That Lawrence did not continue with this novel was by no means due to a loss of interest in the subject, but rather to the fact that Frieda Lawrence put a stop to the collaboration because Mabel Dodge had designs on Lawrence.

And then, for a surprisingly long time, Lawrence put aside the idea of writing an American novel. All that he did immediately in New Mexico, in the way of fiction, was to make numerous changes in *Kangaroo,* including the new last chapter. In November and early December he rewrote his American literature essays. During the latter part of this time he and Frieda were living at Del Monte ranch, high up in the Sangre de Cristo range just below the ranch they were eventually to own, for late in November they had fallen into such disagreement with Mabel Dodge as to abandon her colony. Lawrence spoke often of returning to Europe in the spring, perhaps by way of Mexico, but he said nothing more, for a time, about writing a new novel of the American continent. Besides the revised essays, his attempts to take account of his surroundings in writing were confined to a few poems and to occasional pieces about the Indians. In his remote and wintry landscape he chopped wood and carried on an intentionally simple life, while he looked out over the vast reaches of desert and mountain to the west, the territory of the upper Rio Grande.

But by late February Lawrence was studying Spanish, reading books on Mexico, and making definite plans to go there, saying that he would not soon come home to Europe. It was a periodic shift of feeling with him, and had been since he left Europe, on the one hand that in leaving his home continent he was shirking a responsibility, and on the other that it was only when he was wandering the world that he was in search of his true self.

Lawrence's eventful first journey to Mexico brought him to Mexico City on March 23, 1923. His estimate of the country, in letters, changed by mood. He preferred it to the States, now and again, but he disliked the Aztec carvings he saw in the National Museum. Still, he was deeply impressed by the pyramids at Teotihuacan. He and Frieda drifted around quite a bit, to Cuernavaca, Puebla, Orizaba and other spots, with Witter Bynner and Willard Johnson. Lawrence considered finding a house in or near Mexico City. Then, after a month of uncertainty, he made up his mind to sail from Vera Cruz to New York, but on the very last day, he all at once decided to go and look for a house near Guadalajara. This was what he spoke of as a last effort to remain in Mexico. The upshot was that within a week he had rented a house in Chapala, on the lake of the same name south of Guadalajara.

Here, within a few days of moving in, he began the first version, never yet published, of *The Plumed Serpent*. We may refer to this version as *Quetzalcoatl,* seeing that Lawrence originally gave his novel the name of this Mexican god, and had to be persuaded by his publishers to call it *The Plumed Serpent*. This decision to write an American novel, after a seven-months' delay, was not, however, as impulsive as it may seem. Witter Bynner believed, from Lawrence's manner, that he had writing a novel in mind almost from the start of his visit to Mexico, and Lawrence had written to Amy Lowell, about two weeks before he began: "I would like to sit down and write a novel on the American continent (I don't mean *about* it: I mean while I'm here). But it is hard to break through the wall of the atmosphere."[4] But now the breakthrough had come, and the subject was after all to be America, the revival of its primordial spirit through a religious and political revolution. From the full record that Lawrence left in his letters of most of his doings at the time, as well as from a few other sources, we can reconstruct with reasonable accuracy how Lawrence's American novel grew and changed during a period of nearly two years, and how it found its way into print in 1926.

Frieda Lawrence reports in *Not I, But the Wind . . .* that her husband went every morning to the lakeside to write outdoors, under the trees.[5] There, in his sure and precise handwriting, he filled over 450 pages, in two bound notebooks he had bought in Mexico City, plus a few loose leaves he inserted from another, similar notebook. From sometime around May 15 until past June 20, he worked steadily, ending with something like 150,000 words out of this period of roughly six weeks, or about 3,500 words per day, assuming that he wrote every single day. Whether Lawrence even intended this to be more than a preliminary draft is not altogether clear. He did speak of it as the "first rough form"[6] of the novel, but, as we will see, he went so far as to have it put into typescript, a thing he did not customarily do with a first draft. In any case, as we follow Lawrence's quest for a fictional expression of America, this draft is worth a certain amount of attention.

The first thing we may surmise from it is that while Lawrence knew from the start the general course that his heroine was to follow, he did not know how to incorporate the Indian element of America into his vision, though the impulse to do so went far back into his past. In the Eastwood days he had taken a youthful delight in Cooper, with special fascination, according to Jessie Chambers, for the Great Lakes country settings of the Leatherstocking novels,[7] a fascination which may be traced on down to his rediscovery of Cooper in the middle of the Great War, when he began to see the American Indian as a living example of "the sensual being which for ages [the white man] has been destroying or fleeing from."[8] In his first post-war novel, *The Lost Girl,* Lawrence devised Indian-like masquerades, with nothing to go on still but his own fancy, in order to objectify Alvina Houghton's initiation into a new order of sensual being. By the time of his own arrival in America, Lawrence had not by any means surrendered his concept of the Indian as a living column of blood walking in a mysterious and fecund darkness, but he was more inclined now to be suspicious of such a view. His first observation of Indian ceremonies, at the Jicarilla Apache Reservation in New Mexico, together with all the other new strangeness and color of the Southwest, gave him the uneasy feeling that he might be in the presence of a gigantic masquerade — of the very sort for which he had tried to force a suspension of disbelief in *The Lost Girl* — or else that the Indians of modern America were "up against a dead wall, even more than we are,"[9] survivals of a stage of human culture beyond recovery, to whose drums he could not "cluster" any more.[10] His best efforts, at this Apache ceremony, to see "the nomad nations gathering still in the continent of hemlock trees and prairies,"[11] were not enough to overcome the strong doubts as to the authenticity of this experience informing the same essay. These doubts stand as reason enough for Lawrence's hesitancy in beginning an American novel.

It is at once obvious in *Quetzalcoatl,* however, that Lawrence had made several immediate discoveries about Mexico which to some degree offset his lingering uncertainty with native American themes and offered him the substance to begin his novel. His imagination responded to the debasing of a former Indian culture by such imported corrupt rituals as the bull-fight. He also responded to the politcal turmoil of Mexico, which seemed to make possible almost any sort of revolution: in fact just the kind of modified revival of Aztec culture that Lawrence now attempted to shape, since it was the long suppression of the indigenous spirit which he felt was the cause of the current Mexican unrest. Further, he had discovered a lake, which greeted his imagination as a true geographical symbol of rebirth. This was in keeping both with the fact that the Aztecs had built a lake civilization, and that Chapala resuscitated in him the mystery of lakes, under whose spell he had fallen long ago in knowing Cooper's Glimmerglass. These attractions of Mexico, the ritual, the political, and the geographical, caught such firm and immediate control of Lawrence as to remain essentially the same from *Quetzalcoatl* to *The Plumed Serpent*. It was chiefly the mythic aspects of the fiction, and those rituals of the Southwestern Indians which he knew to be his true source but did not yet thoroughly comprehend, which were to undergo the greatest change from first to last draft of the novel.

The Kate of *Quetzalcoatl* is not, as she is later on, an active seeker, but rather, at the outset, a wanderer. As in *The Plumed Serpent,* she first encounters Don Cipriano Viedma when she is fleeing in disgust from that degraded ceremony, the bull-fight, but though he is dark and, as Lawrence decided in a small revision of the early text, bearded,[12] he strikes Kate as Italian, not Indian. Not until some pages later is he revealed as a pure Mexican Indian. On the other hand, Don Ramón Carrasco, the other principal male of the book, is introduced as totally Indian on his first appearance here, with such a profound hatred of whites that he longs to offer their hearts to the sun, as opposed to the same character in *The Plumed Serpent,* who has little if any indigenous blood, but seems to Kate to represent the oldest spirit of Europe.

This modification points directly to one of Lawrence's changes of purpose between versions of the novel. *Quetzalcoatl* sets up a clearly defined revolution of the native Indian against the tyranny of European culture, even though Ramón's "American Indian" mysticism is deeply imbued with the esoteric doctrines of Europe that Lawrence had learned from Madame Blavatsky and other sources. The revolution in *Quetzalcoatl* is to remedy what has so far been the principal Indian problem: the failure "of a race of men to possess their own souls."[13] *The Plumed Serpent* complicates the matter extensively by turning Ramón, the instigator of the rebellion, into a white man, and there are foreshadowings of this change even in *Quetzalcoatl,* when after his initial appearance Ramón's skin is sometimes described as lighter than at other times. The change between versions reflects the other side of Lawrence's conflicting view of the dark races, instanced by such occasional remarks as "you don't catch me going back on my whiteness."[14] But in *Quetzalcoatl* Ramón's quest for a racial self is nevertheless made more transparently a correlative of Lawrence's own quest for self than in the later version of the novel. The "profound disappointment of an unaccomplished race" is, in Ramón and by inference in Lawrence, grounded in "the misery of a man who has never been able to accomplish his own manhood."[15] And this earlier Ramón, like one facet of Lawrence's own nature, is pleased that Mexico is "masculine." Its gender is masculine in the Romance languages; but also, because of its *machismo,* it permits hope to Cipriano and Ramón that the new religion will be a religion of men, not of priests and women.

Another element of *Quetzalcoatl* that links the Ramón portrayed with Lawrence himself is the complete presentation of Ramón's spiritual struggle to divest himself of all Christian belief, a struggle in which the burning of all the Christian images from the village church at the lake is a crisis of giant porportions, while it is almost purely an act of consummation in *The Plumed Serpent.* It is as if Lawrence, in *Quetzalcoatl,* is reliving a change of heart that took place for him in the Great War, when his rejection of much Christian symbolism for the half-mystical pre-Socratic philosophy of the Greeks nearly coincided with his first envisaging of the American Indian as the bringer of rebirth.

If Lawrence was a long time in clarifying to his own satisfaction his vision of the Indian, he could by the date of working on *Quetzalcoatl* make convincing use of some bits of what he had observed and read. We find here the male and the female rain of the Navajo, the high-pitched singsong of the Apache dancers, the drums and dance-steps and rattles of Taos pueblo, all of which were to be elaborated, later on, by what Lawrence saw and read and pondered during the interval between versions of the novel. This same sort of deepening and expanding was to take place to some extent in the prose rendering of the atmosphere of Mexico. We might expect this from the enlargement of Lawrence's experience with that country, but even in *Quetzalcoatl* the vibrant colors and the marvelous contrast of light and dark, the sort of manifestation of place that Lawrence had long been bringing to pass in his travel books, are already strongly in evidence. And where we will find rituals resembling those of Southwestern Indians in *The Plumed Serpent,* we find in *Quetzalcoatl* many examples that owe much to what Lawrence had witnessed in a few weeks of popular Mexican culture. There is more singing to guitars than to drums in *Quetzal-coatl* — including, as a variation, a lute-like instrument played by Ramón which resembles, from the description, the *conchas* played by the *concheros* of Mexico, dancers whose origin does go back to aboriginal times and whom Lawrence may have seen perform on his first visit to that country.[16]

Two last points may be noted from *Quetzalcoatl* in anticipation of what stands out in the final form of Lawrence's Mexican novel. The political structure Lawrence has in mind in *Quetzalcoatl* oftens appears nearer than in *The Plumed Serpent* to his earlier scheme for an ideal colony, his Rananim. This is particuluarly clear in Ramón's plans for a new system of village life — Lawrence uses the term "commune" here — in which there will be a chief and a chieftainess of peace, the local living Quetzalcoatl and living Malinchi, and the people will produce essentially all they need to live on.[17] The second point is the important development of the nature of Kate from *Quetzalcoatl* to *The Plumed Serpent*. Her active resistance-attraction to the movement of religious and political revival, which takes time to develop in the former, is much strengthened in the latter. The ending of *Quetzalcoatl* is very unsatisfactory indeed in this respect, for Kate merely prepares to sail away and leave it all, pretty much as Lawrence shut the notebooks of his manuscript at the end of June, 1923, in Chapala, and took a train north.

Lawrence said in a letter written right after his arrival in the United States from Mexico, in mid-July, that he would have his manuscript typed in New York: which leaves uncertain exactly what he thought of this early version. He was in and around New York for about a month on this trip, but the typing had not been completed by the time he left again for the West Coast, around August 20, for he asked his current American publisher, Thomas Seltzer, in a letter from Los Angeles on August 31, when he might expect to have the typescript.[18] Actually, it remained in New York all the while Lawrence was in Mexico, and later in Europe, that summer and fall and through the winter of 1923–24. In the last week of February, 1924, Lawrence wrote to Curtis Brown, his agent: "I shall have to go to New York to get that MS. of the Mexican novel — and I must go down to Mexico if I am to finish that book for autumn — so probably I may as well go at once. But I'll talk it over with you."[19] This typescript has survived, now in the possession of Harvard Univerity, as has the Chapala manuscript from which it was made, which is held in the Humanities Research Center at the University of Texas. Lawrence retrieved both manuscript and typescript as he passed through New York from England on his way to New Mexico, in March, 1924.

He began making changes in the typescript either in Taos or else in Mexico, where he did not go until the fall of that year. The typescript of *Quetzalcoatl* is 360 pages long, but after page 203, except for a few changes of the name of Kate's servant from the real name of her original to Felipa, Lawrence did no revising on the text, not even to correct obvious errors, so that his decision to abandon *Quetzalcoatl* and start over was made after he had re-examined about half of his previous work. This decision he apparently made in Oaxaca, just when he was ready to get down to work, at least according to Dorothy Brett: "You take up your writing. You read what you have written in Chapala of *The Plumed Serpent*.

"'I will have to rewrite it,' you say. 'Chapala has not really the spirit of Mexico, it is too tamed, too touristy. This place is more untouched.'"[20]

Before we take up the composition of the definitive *Plumed Serpent,* however, we must give some attention to the events of the middle months of 1924, which had such a profound effect on the novel. On the day in April when he arrived back in Taos, Lawrence was already planning to stay long enough to see an Easter dance at San Felipe or Santo Domingo.[21] He attended the spring corn dance at Santo Domingo later in the month, and the Hopi snake dance also, in August. The rain ceremony entirely new to the ultimate *Plumed Serpent* is based on these. The circular dance in the plaza of Sayula into which Kate is drawn soon after her arrival, also new to the later version of the novel, may have had its origin in Lawrence's earliest observation of Taos dances, but the scene also has strong echoes of the dances the Taos Indians engaged in at their nightly campfire under the pine trees after their day's work on the cabins at Kiowa Ranch, in the spring of 1924. The Lawrences had acquired this ranch and hired the Indians to help prepare the cabins for summer residence. Lawrence wrote his "Pan in America," or much of it, within the sound of those drums, a piece that expresses a crucial stage in his growing understanding of what he would later fashion into rituals in the novel. Lawrence did a great deal of reading on Indians during that summer, too, which gave final form, for instance, to the "origin myth" to which Kate listens just before the dance in the plaza scene mentioned above, a feature also new to *The Plumed Serpent*.

In another re-adjustment of purpose, not an addition this time but a subtraction, Lawrence transferred the original concept of the Indian retaking America by his own effort, and not under the leadership of a white man, to "The Woman Who Rode Away," one of the three great pieces of short fiction he wrote in the summer of 1924. Here he did imitate Indian dances he had known previously, the winter dances of Taos, and he based the story on a belief supposedly prevalent in the Southwest. This is how it reads in *Quetzalcoatl*: "Kate thought of the Indians of the northern pueblos. They believe with such devilish certainty that the wheel of fate will bring the end of the white man's day, that the white man will perish from the earth, and the Red Man will be the world's lord."[22] All three of these 1924 stories — "The Princess" and "St. Mawr" besides "The Woman Who Rode Away" — take up the life-and-death struggles of questing women to put themselves right with a powerful, fearful yet potentially redeeming male spirit, a spirit of the landscape comprised of American mountains, partly Southwestern and partly Mexican. The stories were a preparation for the final assult that Lawrence was soon to make on creating his imaginary continent.

We now come, then, to consider the only texts representing truly Lawrence's final aims in writing his American novel, and the only ones demanding close scrutiny for the establishing of an authentic text of *The Plumed Serpent*. These are the holograph manuscript of the last stage of the writing, which like the first reposes in the Humanities Research Center in Austin, and the typescript made from this holograph, located in the same library.

Lawrence left Taos in early October, 1924, with Frieda and with Dorothy Brett, by now a confirmed disciple. He had already said that he wished to go deeper into the Mexico of the Indian than the Chapala region, and had mentioned Oaxaca as a possibility, the land of the Mixtecs and the Zapotecs. Within a month of setting out, he and the two women had arrived in Oaxaca, the Lawrences had taken a house to themselves, and he was ready to resume the task that had been in abeyance for well over a year. The day after moving into the house, on November 24, 1924, he began a completely new manuscript in one of two new copybooks. After his usual fashion, he wrote rapidly once he was under way. He had filled the three hundred and eighty-one pages of the first notebook with the first twelve chapters and the start of the thirteenth of his novel by December 31, that is to say, in six weeks, and had commenced on the second notebook, which carried him through page 758 of his manuscript, running from the last part of Chapter XIII on through to the beginning sections of Chapter XXV. Not having much to go to end the novel, and perhaps not having a new notebook at hand, Lawrence picked up the second notebook of the first *Quetzalcoatl*, went to the several blank leaves at the back, turned the book upside down and entered the last 39 pages of his work therein, corresponding to the latter section of Chapter XXV and all of Chapter XXVI. He was "nearly done" with the whole novel, he said, by January 16, 1925.[23] On January 29, he wrote that he was on the last chapter.[24]

From this point on a number of textual intricacies arise due to a drastic turn of events in Lawrence's life. As he was writing the closing pages of *The Plumed Serpent* he was struck by the worst illness, so far, of his life, an attack of tuberculosis, according to a German doctor he later consulted in Mexico City. It we can take literally what he said to Amy Lowell over two months later, in early April, 1925, when he was back in New Mexico and slowly mending, he took the manuscript to be finished at the time he fell sick, and in fact connected the two events: "I managed to finish my novel *Quetzalcoatl* in Mexico: the very day I went down, as if shot in the intestines. But I daren't even look at the outside of the MS. It cost one so much. . . ."[25] On this manuscript itself Lawrence never did make many changes. Only a few words or at most a few lines are crossed out and written above here and there, with some other interlinear additions and one or two changes of chapter titles. But any or all of these particular alterations may have come about the the manuscript grew in Oaxaca. It was not really until Lawrence had a complete typescript that he made important revisions.

There are a great many gaps in what I have so far been able to piece together of when, where and by whom the typing of the manuscript was accomplished. Dorothy Brett says in *Lawrence and Brett* that she did some typing of *The Plumed Serpent* manuscript in Oaxaca. She left there a few weeks ahead of the Lawrences but not long before he had finished his manuscript. She mentioned working hard to finish all she could before she departed, but she was not a rapid typist and it is thus improbable that she came near to finishing a typescript of the whole novel.[26] Lawrence does not mention a text which is identifiable as a typescript until April 21, when he was still loathing the thought of having to go over his novel "to prune and correct, in typescript."[27] And even then he did not indicate whether as yet he had a typescript in hand. It appears, from remarks dropped here and there in the letters, that he had sent the holograph manuscript to Curtis Brown's New York office to be typed—Curtis Brown, his English agent, had recently taken over his American affairs as well, and any former understanding with the publisher Thomas Seltzer, who had seen to the typing of *Quetzalcoatl,* was now off, for Seltzer was on the verge of bankruptcy and Lawrence was trying to get free of him. The faithful Dorothy Brett was in Taos, and although she did a substantial amount of typing for Lawrence in the spring and summer of 1925, she ordinarily identifies to some degree what she was typing, and she does not mention working on *The Plumed Serpent* at this time. She did type the first piece of work Lawrence turned out when he again felt up to writing, the play *David,* most of which Lawrence wrote during the month of May while he was still reluctant to return to his novel.

But at last, around June 1, he did turn to it, and he was busy at revisions for nearly a whole month. He had, it appears, one entire and one partial typescript to work with, and in a fashion that is not wholly to be reconstructed on the basis of present evidence, he produced a revised text which was surely in essence the present Texas typescript, only with some pages typed over later on. One of the several oddities of this text is the numbering of the pages. For the first 118 pages, that is, through the end of Chapter V, the numbering is consecutive. From here on, for the remaining twenty-two chapters (the holograph manuscript contains only twenty-six chapters, but in the typescript Chapter XII was divided into two chapters during final revision), the pages of each chapter are numbered separately. It is also at the end of Chapter V that a change of typewriters took place. Why Lawrence made use of part of two different typescripts, when he probably had a whole one before him from his agent, I have not to this point been able to determine. The consecutively numbered typescript did in fact continue beyond Chapter V, at least through Chapter VI and part of Chapter VII, for such a fragment is now in the Berkeley library. A comparison of these pages with the overlapping section of the Texas typescript shows that each text came directly and independently from the holograph manuscript at the same stage of revision in the text. The Berkeley fragment also has holograph corrections, but these often differ from those appearing in the Texas typescript, which shows that Lawrence worked on each one independently. Ernest Tedlock speaks of a carbon copy of part of the Berkeley fragment on which Lawrence has made corrections differing still from those in the Berkeley text.[28]

With at least three separate approaches to revision before us, it is obvious that Lawrence lavished much care on the final text of *The Plumed Serpent*. He may not have gotten down to the revising with the thought that he might spend a month on it, or almost half the time he had taken to write the last manuscript draft, for on June 10 he reported that he had revised the novel as if the task were finished. But then he must have changed his mind, for on June 23 he informed Curtis Brown that he expected to be through by the following week, and mention of the subject again in a letter of June 29 suggests that the book was now truly done.[29] Lawrence was working on a text for which there was more or less a duplicate in New York, probably a carbon copy retained there awaiting his revisions on an original which had been mailed to him. This is made clear by this report to Martin Secker, the prospective London publisher, on June 18: "I will send this revised MS.

to New York, to Curtis Brown, and when they've made all the alterations in the duplicate, I'll tell them to let you see it."[30]

There is still nothing in this to explain the substitution of a different typescript for the first five chapters of what was apparently a whole typescript from the agent, and other puzzles remain as well. For instance, there is a section at the end of the book, of several pages, which is practically unrevised in the holograph manuscript but which yet was rejected by Lawrence, for the ending in the typescript is completely different. What happened to the revised text from which the typescript was obviously made I cannot say. The most likely explanation is that Lawrence so heavily revised such pages as this in the typescript from his agent that when this arrived back in New York a typist did the pages over rather than entering the changes on the "duplicate," and there are several pieced-in partial pages in the defiinitive typescript to support this hypothesis. In any case, it was from this composite typescript that the novel was printed, and for arriving at an authentic text, this is the most important single fact.

Lawrence submitted the corrected typescript of *The Plumed Serpent* to Curtis Brown's New York office around July 1, 1925, already all but sure that Alfred Knopf would be publishing it in the United States and Martin Secker in England. He was hopeful that the printing process might soon begin, for he wished to send a set of galleys to G. R. C. Conway in Mexico City, a man whose opinion on Mexican lore he valued. Apparently there was no time for this, in light of all that I can gather from the progress made in bringing the novel to print. In these final stages a new group of interesting and sometimes perplexing problems arose which will call for a great deal of judicious choice in the process of critical editing.

Both Knopf and Secker had decided to accept the novel, but Lawrence may not have seen the galleys when he came through New York on his way to England in September. He sent some galleys back to Knopf on the day he sailed, but it is not certain these were for the novel. Probably they were for the essay of Lawrence's that was to appear in Knopf's *Borzoi Book,* published in December, 1925.[31]

What is curious, later on, is to find Lawrence treating galley corrections the way he did in England. In mid-October, probably on the 16th, he wrote Martin Secker from his sister's home in Derbyshire to say that Galley #156 was missing from the set he was then engaged in correcting and to ask that it be sent immediately. Presumably he received it. He had plans to leave Derbyshire on the following Wednesday, the 20th, and on that day he had finished his galleys, for he wrote as follows to the Knopfs: "I've sent the proofs of *The Plumed Serpent* back to Secker, so you should have a revised set very soon now."[32] Lawrence was thus handling galley revisions as he had on the typescript: he entered changes on one copy and returned it for these to be transferred to any other necessary copy in the office concerned.

The odd thing here is that while the sending of corrected galleys from London to New York would ordinarily indicate that both publishers were somehow involved in an identical printing operation, this was not the case at all: there was, for instance, no selling of sheets by one publisher to another, as was often the practice between American and British publishing houses. Knopf's first American edition was set up by the Vailballou Press in Binghamton, New York, and Secker's first English edition by the Dunedin Press Limited in Edinburgh. Why, then, did Lawrence have a set of Secker galleys, with his corrections copied in, mailed off to Knopf? Perhaps because of time. Galleys from Knopf's printer would have taken a long time to come from America and be returned. To add to the delay, Lawrence did not mean to remain in England for very long, but to go on to Italy, or even to Yugoslavia, where the mails were uncertain. Knopf of course wanted to publish as soon as possible — he did bring the novel out on January 15, 1926, only three months after Lawrence informed him that galleys incorporating his final corrections were on the way: a short time given the habitual slowness of printers. What must have happened, then, is that a set of galleys from Secker, with Lawrence's final changes copied in at Secker's office, was dispatched to Knopf. Then in New York the changes were transferred to galleys from the Vailballou Press by someone in Knopf's office and these were returned to the American printer as final working copy.

This makes, to be sure, for a considerable entanglement of revisions and the consequent difficulties in collation. But there are, at the same time, attendant advantages. We know, for one thing, that Lawrence oversaw the printing of his novel in England up through the last phase in which an author is ordinarily consulted, the galley phase. And the choice of a copytext is thus made easy. By the time corrected galleys reached the American printer, the changes in them were twice removed from the author's hand, with the inevitable creeping in of errors. It is safe to assume that Secker retained for his own use the galleys that Lawrence himself had corrected, and thus the first English edition should be the text least subject to mistakes, having issued more directly than any other under the supervision of the author. Unfortunately, however, none of these corrected galleys have apparently survived. However, two sets of uncorrected galleys are extant.

From the foregoing reconstruction of Lawrence's task in writing his American novel and the fortunes of various manuscripts on their way to publication, it is apparent that a great deal of editorial work will be necessary in establishing a definitive text. Since I propose here only the beginning of the project, some changes in the procedure to be outlined may prove essential. But so far at least, the undertaking may be summed up as follows. The greatest single task will be a sight collation of the five known major texts: the Oaxaca holograph manuscript, the definitive typescript made from this, the uncorrected galleys, the first English edition, and the first American edition: with the first English edition serving, to repeat, as the copy-text. And while the greater portion of the work will be carried out in this way, from photographic reproductions, certain difficulties are bound to arise which can only be settled by consulting the original texts themselves, a requirement simplified by the fact that all the major texts are housed at the Humanities Research Center, University of Texas at Austin, and can thus be compared together all at once.

Apart from the sight collation of the five main texts and such fragments as may turn up, there should be one further stage of collation, that of two or more representative copies of the same printing of the novel, especially important, of course, for the first English edition, since this is to be the copy-text. Fortunately, this stage of collation can be effected mechanically, by Hinman collator, and will not unduly tax the patience of the editor and his assistants. This latter collation should be viewed as a precaution rather than a step which is likely to yield many textual changes. Some printings of the two 1926 editions after the first were made during Lawrence's lifetime, but so far as can be determined at this time, no alterations were made in these in which the author intervened. Other later editions of *The Plumed Serpent* exist as well, of course, but all these were published after Lawrence's death in 1930 and constitute no authority in the establishing of a definitive text.

Beyond the matter of an authoritative text, another question arises as to what is essential to assist the ordinary educated reader in comprehending Lawrence's artistic intention. This is a question that stems from the specific historical and cultural circumstances that helped to inspire the novel. Lawrence wrote *The Plumed Serpent* while thinking about events of the Mexican Revolution, with many allusions to contemporary happenings in Mexico and assumed knowledge on the part of his readers then that readers this half-century later will no longer possess. He also drew on native American mythology little known to most readers of the Anglo-Saxon world. It seems therefore necessary to include, in an up-to-date edition of this particular novel of Lawrence's, two special appendices, one on the political scene in Mexico in the twenties, another on the mythology of which he made use.

Lawrence's psychological and artistic association with America was a highly complex matter, and so, as we have seen, were his endeavors to put his vision into the form of a novel. This situation will call for a well-informed judgment in the matter of substantives, for cases are bound to arise in which no absolute proof exists as to the author's ultimate intention, with no way left to reach a decision except by the exercise of the best principles of textual criticism. An interesting example of Lawrence's constantly changing viewpoint is the ending of the novel, although in this particular case he makes the textual choice easy for his editor. It was not until the last minute that Lawrence could determine how to end *The Plumed Serpent,* whether to have his heroine go back to Europe or stay and commit herself to the revival of the aboriginal religion. Kate was merely packing to leave, we remember, at the end of *Quetzalcoatl.* At the end of the Oaxaca manuscript, Don Ramón sends her back to Europe as a sort of missionary, but warns that she will have little success and charges her to return to Mexico when the attempt at the conversion of Europe is over. In the Texas typescript Kate succeeds in getting Don Cipriano, now her husband both by civil ceremonies and those of the new religion, to beg her to stay, but Lawrence did not succeed in presenting the whole interplay of these attraction-rejection motives until he was correcting the galleys, when he changed the last sentence of the book to give it the force of these motives, which it so very aptly does, while none of the previous experiments in an ending had done so.

Lawrence seldom ended fictional situations by resolving them fully. More often than not they lead on to other life-questions, and this is what the ending of *The Plumed Serpent* does. Lawrence remarked about his fiction, when he was storing up emotional strength to write the ultimate version of this novel, "It's got to be lived out: not thought out."[33] The pitch of involvement with living to which he brings Kate Leslie can do no more than reflect his own forever intense but never fully resolved attraction-repulsion attitude toward America.

*Notes:*

1. Mabel Dodge Luhan, *Lorenzo in Taos* (New York: Alfred A. Knopf, 1935), p. 24.

2. D. H. Lawrence, *Kangaroo* (New York: The Viking Press, Compass edition, 1960), p. 359.

3. ———, *Phoenix* (London: William Heinemann Ltd., 1936), p. 142.

4. S. Foster Damon, *Amy Lowell: A Chronicle* (Boston and New York: Houghton Mifflin Co., 1935), p. 638.

5. Frieda Lawrence, *Not I, But the Wind . . .* (New York: The Viking Press, 1934), p. 139.

6. D. H. Lawrence, *Collected Letters,* ed. Harry T. Moore (New York: The Viking Press, 1962), II, 742.

7. Jessie Chambers, *D. H. Lawrence: A Personal Record* (London: Frank Cass Ltd., 1965), p. 96.

8. D. H. Lawrence, *The Symbolic Meaning: Uncollected Versions of Studies in Classic American Literature* (Fontinell, Arundel: The Centaur Press Ltd., 1962), p. 110.

9. ———, *Collected Letters,* Moore edition, II, 721.

10. *Phoenix,* p. 99.

11. *Phoenix,* p. 94.

12. D. H. Lawrence, "Quetzalcoatl" (an unpublished typescript deposited in the Houghton Library, Harvard University), p. 14.

13. "Quetzalcoatl," p. 56.

14. *Collected Letters,* Moore edition, II, 702.

15. "Quetzalcoatl," p. 134.

16. "Quetzalcoatl," p. 106.

17. "Quetzalcoatl," pp. 239–40.

18. Gerald M. Lacy, "An Analytical Calendar of the Letters of D. H. Lawrence," Diss., University of Texas at Austin, 1971, p. 320.

19. *The Letters of D. H. Lawrence,* ed. and with an introduction by Aldous Huxley (London: William Heinemann Ltd., 1932), p. 596.

20. Dorothy Brett, *Lawrence and Brett* (Philadelphia: J. B. Lippincott Co., 1933), p. 181.

21. Lacy, p. 341.

22. "Quetzalcoatl," p. 109.

23. Damon, p. 670.

24. D. H. Lawrence, *Letters to Martin Secker, 1911–1930* (Buckingham, England: Martin Secker, 1970), p. 62.

25. *Letters,* Moore edition, II, 833.

26. Brett, p. 207.

27. *Letters,* Moore edition, II, 140.

28. E. W. Tedlock, Jr., *The Frieda Lawrence Collection of D. H. Lawrence Manuscripts: A Descriptive Bibliography* (Albuquerque: University of New Mexico Press, 1948), p. 18.

29. Letters, Moore edition, II, 843–45; D. H. Lawrence, *The Centaur Letters* (Austin: Humanities Research Center, 1970), p. 20.

30. *Letters to Martin Secker,* p. 62.

31. Lacy, p. 379.

32. *Letters,* Moore edition, II, 860.

33. *Letters,* Moore edition, II, 761.

*White House Ruin: Canyon de Chelly National Monument, Arizona, by Ansel Adams from* Photographs of the Southwest, *New York Graphic Society, Boston, Mass.*

# A CHRONOLOGY OF LCP KEEPSAKES

## Al Lowman

BIBLIOPHILES IN AND OUT OF LIBRARIES long have been interested in the literary assessments of Lawrence Clark Powell. In the realm of reading and learning he has been an exceedingly influential critic and tastemaker through his multiple roles as librarian, teacher, essayist, and popular speaker.

The world knows that he enjoys good writing. He also likes to see it in attractive format and then to share it with others. To that end he has, for many years, commissioned printing craftsmen on the West Coast and in Europe to create keepsakes that he has distributed privately on special occasions. At times Powell himself has authored these pamphlets and leaflets, especially when he has wished to commemorate the life and work of cherished friends. At other moments he simply has been amused, moved, or exhilarated by something he has read and has had the urge to preserve it in a setting worthy of its quality.

The printer who has most frequently assisted Powell in his schemes is Will Cheney, with whom he began collaborating in 1951. Together they are responsible for eleven items in this checklist. To the association of Powell and Ward Ritchie may be attributed five, including the very earliest ones. Four imprints, completed between 1959 and 1966, were produced in the Netherlands — three of them by N. V. Drukkerij Trio.

Taken together this collection of some three dozen pieces displays irresistable combination of forms, balance, proportion, color, harmony, contrast, tone, and texture — all the elements needed to create things of beauty.

If Shakespeare distrusted the man with no music in his soul, then I place no greater assurance in the man who fails to cherish the printed word in appropriate guise. Larry Powell obviously feels the same. We are grateful for the pleasure he has shared.

NOTE: *Place of issue is Los Angeles, unless otherwise indicated*

## 1939

[1] Powell, Lawrence Clark (ed.). *H. Clark Powell, 1900–1938.* Memoirs of his life and a Bibliography of his Writings. 18 pages. Deckled edges. 20.1 cm x 12.8 cm. Issued in both wrappers and boards.

"125 copies printed by the Ward Ritchie Press." — From the colophon. Twenty-five were bound in blue-gray boards with black cloth spine and printed title label, while the remainder were hand-tied in blue-gray wrappers.

Harold Clark Powell, oldest of three Powell brothers, became an eminent horticulturalist at Pretoria in the South African commonwealth. His untimely death from an accidental fall prompted this memorial volume.

Its design befits a man of restrained and reflective personality. Janson is the only typeface used, and the paper is linweave text with deckled edges. The endsheets of the hardbound copies are of the same stock, which contributes to the book's unity. Ornamentation is limited to the classical title page where discreet printers' flowers enhance the typography, and to the unobtrusive brackets which enclose the folios.

The booklet is further enhanced with two striking photographs — a frontis portrait of H. Clark Powell and a view of the Pretorious Kop in the Kruger National Park where his ashes were scattered. These were printed from collotypes made at the Meridan Gravure Company. Adrian Wilson has noted that "collotype, or photogelatin printing, is now produced by only a few companies in the world, but the process is still unsurpassed for rendering the finest details of art and photography." — *The Design of Books.* 54.

## 1940

[2] Powell, Gertrude Clark. *A Little Tour to Vézelay.* [10] pages, plus colophon leaf. Deckled edges. 19.1 cm x 14.1 cm. Hand-tied in rust-colored wrappers.

"75 copies for Gertrude Clark Powell on her 70th birthday, October 18, 1940, from her brother, Harold, her sister, Marian, and her sons, George and Lawrence. Printed by the Ward Ritchie Press." — From the colophon.

This was an excerpt from Mrs. Powell's manuscript *The Quiet Side of Europe,* finally published in 1959. [See item 21.] The text of this pamphlet may be found on pages 98-103 of the book.

The summer of 1932 was an idyllic one for Mrs. Powell, filled with joyous excursions into the Burgundian countryside. Particularly memorable for her was a tour to the venerable hamlet of Vézelay and its magnificent church, the Basilique de la Madeline, some sixty-five miles northwest of Dijon. A visit to the church, a stroll to the *terérasse,* and refreshment at a café on the *place* completed an adventure that ended too quickly. "Nightfall found us home in Dijon, with memories of one of our happiest days in France."

This pamphlet is a superior and enduring example of the printer's art. The favorable first impression of color, paper, and texture is sustained by the subtle typographical lead-in to the text. The title only is delicately printed in 8-point Janson caps on the front cover and is repeated on the half title. The title page itself develops a warm strength. The single illustration, which precedes the text, is a *Life* magazine photograph of Vézelay dominated by its great basilica. Powell obtained permission to reproduce it from Henry R. Luce. The text is set in 12-point Janson and is printed on a fine, laid paper. Thus the sharp and thin serifs characteristic of that face take on added color, making the printing even fuller and richer.

## 1945

[3] Pepys, Samuel. *A Pepysian Pastorale.* 6 pages plus colophon leaf. Deckled edges. 17.8 cm x 12.8 cm. Hand-tied in dark green, double-fold wrappers.

"75 copies for Gertrude Clark Powell on her 75th birthday, October 18, 1945, of this excerpt from the Diary of her favorite writer from her son Lawrence and his wife Fay. Printed by Richard Hoffman."

The output of Hoffman, Los Angeles printer and teacher, is distinguished by immaculate presswork and the restrained use of color. Quite often the page numerals are lightened with attractive ornaments, as in this keepsake.

The perfection of the title page is fractionally diminished by an oversized decoration, but the printer has nonetheless amplified Pepy's words with boldness and clarity in an utterly congenial format.

[4] Storm, Theodore. *Oktoberlied.* English Translation by C. F. MacIntyre. 7 pages plus colophon leaf. 15.7 cm x 11.4 cm. Hand-tied in cream-colored, double-fold wrappers.

"200 copies printed by the Ward Ritchie Press for the friends of Fay and Lawrence Powell." — From the colophon. Designed by Joseph Simon.

Keen sensitivity in the choice and handling of type is readily demonstrated on the title page where three different faces are successfully integrated. Only the pagination is unduly emphasized by being spelled out within brackets.

## 1946

[5] Longus. *A Winter Pastorale.* 15 pages. 15 cm x 9.7 cm. Hand-tied in light-gray wrappers.

"Of this excerpt from book III of Longus's *Daphnis & Chloe,* translated by George Thornley in 1657, fifty copies have been printed by Grant Dahlstrom at the Castle Press in Pasadena at the time of the winter solstice for the friends of Larry Powell." — From the colophon.

The William Andrews Clark Memorial Library, which Powell served as director, has one of two known copies of Thornley's translation. The title page of 1657 is reproduced here as an illustration preceding the text of this extract. It was one of the first instances in which a picture of a printing press appears on the title page, although Joseph Moxon's later use of this device is better known.

The designer's contribution to this keepsake recalls Ward Ritchie's appraisal of Dahlstrom: "[He] began, like Minerva, in complete maturity, and his very first efforts show the intelligent good taste which has characterized all of his subsequent work." — *A Bookman's View of Los Angeles*, 51.

[6] MacIntyre, C. F. *Judean Slumber Song*. 13.6 cm x 10.7 cm. French-fold.

Although not so stated, this Christmas greeting for Fay and Lawrence Powell was printed by Ward Ritchie. The verse is simply and tastefully framed in a delicate green border mounted with decorative printers' ornaments.

MacIntyre, "a poet and bohemian," was on the Occidental College faculty during Powell's freshman year. He is recalled by L.C.P. as "the most exciting, provocative, stimulating teacher of literature I have ever known." — *Fortune & Friendship*, 15.

[7] Marvell, Andrew. *To His Coy Mistress*. [3] pages plus colophon. Deckled edges. 22 cm x 14 cm. Hand-tied in wrappers.

"75 copies of this poem first issued in 1681 have been reprinted by Reuben Pearson for the friends of Lawrence Clark Powell at Los Angeles, California, 1946." — From the colophon.

The Dutch paper on which this keepsake was printed bears the special watermark of William Andrews Clark, Jr. According to Powell, "When I became director [of the Clark Library] I found a cache of it . . . and we sometimes used it for projects such as this.

"Pearson was a student assistant at the Clark who went on to Columbia for an M.A. in English and is now a high school teacher in Monterey, California." — L.C.P. to A.L. 12-29-73.

The printer's unaffected use of graceful ornaments and borders on beautiful, laid paper summons a romantic atmosphere wholly appropriate to Marvell's lyric. Copies were issued in wrappers of variant colors: gray, cream, and green.

1947

[8] Hillyer, Anthony (pseud. of Thomas Perry Stricker). *Elizabeth's Merlin*. 31 pages. Deckled edges. 17.9 cm x 10.1 cm. Hand-tied in light beige wrappers.

"150 copies printed by Gordon Holmquist for members of the Rounce and Coffin Club and the Typophiles and other friends of the author." — From the colophon.

Instigated by L.C.P. with his "Note" at the end of the text. This was the posthumous completion of three *Tudor Grotesques*, all written by Thomas Perry Stricker as sales descriptions for Jake Zeitlin, and the first two of which were also printed by him. See *Stricker Checklist*, 44.

1948

[9] Anon. *The Holly and the Ivy*. 19.7 cm x 13.4 cm. French-fold.

"For the friends of Lawrence, Fay, Norman and Wilkie Powell. Printed at Christmas 1948 by Richard Hoffman." — From the colophon.

The strength of this keepsake is in the original and inviting front cover design. Inside, stanzas of the poem are printed alternately in red, black, and green. Decorations are used not for ostentation, but with obvious relationship to the typographical scheme.

[10] Powell, Lawrence Clark. *Giacomo Giralamo Casanova: Chevalier de Seingalt, 1725-1798*. Pasadena: The Ampersand Press. 23 pages. 12.2 cm x 8 cm. Brick red, double-fold wrappers.

"In somewhat different form this essay by Lawrence Clark Powell was originally read at a meeting of the Zamorano Club of Los Angeles in March 1947 and has now been printed by Grant Dahlstrom at the Ampersand Press in Pasadena for members of the Club and other friends of the author and the printer." — From the preface.

The Ampersand Press is the imprint occasionally used by Dahlstrom for privately printed books. This appealing miniature is impeccably well designed and produced in a classical treatment that leaves no second thoughts whatever.

1949

[11] Durrell, Lawrence. *A Landmark Gone*. Pages i–ii, [1]–7 plus colophon. 20.4 cm x 13.2 cm. Hand-tied in blue-green wrappers with printed paper label.

"125 copies printed by Reuben Pearson with the author's permission for the friends of Lawrence Clark Powell. 'A Landmark Gone' was first published in *Middle East Anthology,* London, 1964." — From the colophon.

Powell was first a reader and collector of Durrell's poetry and then of his prose contributions long before *The Alexandria Quartet* brought him world-wide attention.

Of this particular keepsake Powell has written, "In 1949 I had a printer friend make a little presentation volume of Durrell's account of his escape from Greece ahead of the Germans." This reprint also contains "A Note on Lawrence Durrell" by L.C.P. It has been reproduced with rare discrimination on a fine Strathmore paper (Alexandra Brilliant) that is no longer obtainable.

[12] MacIntyre, C. F. *Autumn Tithes*. 22.8 cm x 15.5 cm. French-fold.

"One hundred copies printed by Grant Dahlstrom at the Castle Press in Pasadena on October 3, 1949, for members of the Roxburghe Club of San Francisco and other friends of Larry Powell." — From the colophon.

This poem has been printed on a light, cream-colored paper within a thin, double-ruled border. The type is Arrighi italic, with a Centaur initial. Although green is sometimes a dubious choice for a second color, it has been used with compelling effect for both the border and the initial letter.

[13] Rossetti, D. G. *Silent Moon*. 16.5 cm x 12 cm. Single-fold leaflet.

"Poetry Leaflet Number One. Set up in battered type and printed late one night by Frank Jacobson and Reuben Pearson, August, 1949. A few struck off for Larry Powell because he suggested the poem." — From the colophon.

The total edition was thirty copies, of which ten were given to Powell. The colophon of the remaining twenty does not have the reference to Powell.

The format is unpretentious yet tasteful. The need for haste probably dictated repetition of the cover title on the title page.

1951

[14] Lee, Laurie. *An Obstinate Exile*. 14 pages plus colophon leaf. 13.7 cm x 8.7 cm. Tan wrappers.

"One hundred and one copies handset, printed & bound by W. M. Cheney for the friends of Fay Ellen and Lawrence Clark Powell at or near Christmas 1951."— From the colophon.

Originally given as a talk on the BBC, Lee's essay later appeared in *The Listener* from which it was reprinted by Cheney for the Powells. The present issue contains an introductory "Note" by L.C.P.

This keepsake was the first collaboration between Powell and printer Cheney and is an exquisite example of the latter's art.

1952

[15] Lee, Laurie. *City of the Sun*. 13 pages. 20.3 cm x 13.8 cm. Gold wrappers.

"With the permission of the author and of the British Broadcasting Corporation 150 copies were printed by W. M. Cheney for Lawrence Clark Powell to give to his fellow members of the Rounce and Coffin and Zamorano Clubs of Los Angeles and the Roxburghe Club of San Francisco in the autumn of 1952." — From the colophon.

While living under London's drab skies from 1950–52, Powell came across Laurie Lee's description of a day in Ecija, a town of "decayed and gilded splendour," situated between Seville and Cordoba. Lee's prose greatly impressed L.C.P., then homesick for his own desert Southwest. On his return to Los Angeles, he commissioned Cheney to make this printing from *The Listener,* May 22, 1952.

The Baskerville typeface is admirably suited to the author's thoroughly British background, while the vivid gold wrappers with red ornaments evokes the sunburned Spanish countryside. This sense of place is subtly reinforced with ornaments in yellow on the title page, around the initial letter of the text, and again at the end of the text. Cheney's outstanding design won for this pamphlet a place in the 1953 Western Books Exhibit of the Rounce and Coffin Club.

1956

[16] Frugé, August. *Books Are Still For Sale*. 9 pages plus colophon leaf. 11.5 cm x 7.5 cm. Hand-tied in brick red wrappers.

"190 copies privately printed from the *Saturday Review of Literature* for Lawrence Clark Powell by W. M. Cheney." — From the colophon.

Here is a most desirable miniature created from nothing more than the virtuoso employment of typefaces.

[17] Zamorano, Don Agustín Vicente. *The Hand of Zamorano.* A facsimile reproduction of a manuscript on the Californias in 1829. Translated by Arnulfo D. Trejo and Roland D. Hussey. Preface by George L. Harding. Pages i–iv, 1–[15] plus colophon. Deckled edges. 31.5 cm x 22 cm. Hand-tied in beige wrappers.

"250 copies printed by Saul & Lillian Marks at the Plantin Press." — From the colophon.

This pamphlet, honoring California's first printer, was sponsored by the Zamorano Club of Los Angeles as a momento of its third joint meeting with the Roxburghe Club of San Francisco. It was instigated by Powell, then president of the Zamoranans, who found the holograph in a collection of Mexican manuscripts given the UCLA Library by Dr. Rosenbach in 1929.

The resulting keepsake is printed in Bembo, a face derived from the roman letter cut by Francisco Griffo for Aldus Manutius and first used in Cardinal Bembo's *De Aetna* published in 1495. In its modern version it became a hallmark of the Plantin Press. Here it is used with more vivacity and sinew than usual in Plantin Press items, which habitually exemplify grace and elegance.

## 1957

[18] Ashurst, Henry Fountain. *Up in Coconino County.* Pages from the Journal of The Honorable Henry Fountain Ashurst. United States Senator from Arizona, 1912–1941. Pasadena: The Castle Press. 5 pages plus colophon. 23.5 cm x 15.2 cm. Hand-tied in light gray wrappers.

"Eighty-three copies of these pages printed by Grant Dahlstrom as a present to Senator Ashurst on his 83rd birthday, September 13, 1957, from a friend and admirer in Southern California. They were copied out originally by Mr. Ashurst in 1926 for the University of Arizona Library and are printed here for the first time by permission." — From the colophon.

The paper on which this mellifluous title was printed has an earthy yet warm tone that evokes the Southwest. The mood is further enhanced with a title line printed in terra cotta. Utilizing the simplest of typographical elements Grant Dahlstrom has fashioned a printer's classic.

## 1958

[19] Highet, Gilbert. *The Springs of Clitumnus.* 8 pages plus colophon leaf. Deckled edges. 18.5 cm x 11.7 cm. Hand-tied in cream-colored wrappers.

"Forty-five copies printed by W. M. Cheney for L.C.P. with permission of the author and the Oxford University Press, publishers of *Poets in a Landscape,* from which the excerpt comes." — From the colophon.

Designed without ornamentation and featuring only the adroit use of type, Cheney produced an austerely beautiful work that seems to fulfill Beatrice Warde's ideal of printing with crystal goblet clarity.

[20] Powell, Lawrence Clark. *The Southwest Broadsides.* Printed for the Friends of Lawrence Clark Powell, 1953–1958. Pages i–iv, 1–12 plus colophon leaf. 18.3 cm x 11.2 cm. Hand-tied in light gray wrappers.

"Just enough copies were printed by W. M. Cheney to give to those recipients of the Broadsides who said they liked them." — From the colophon.

"I do not recall what it was exactly that inspired this series, other than a state of excitement engendered in me by a trip to Tucson in April, 1953. . . . Over the next five years I chose these texts and printers, and gave the results to my friends and favorite libraries. They prove only that I like good writing about the Southwest in beautiful format and like to share it with others." — From the preface.

A unique design feature of this pamphlet is the vertical, rather than horizontal, use of the Bodoni dash to delineate its various sections.

The individual broadsides in the series are as follows:

A. *A Man Is at His Best* by Will Levington Comfort. Printed by W. M. Cheney, Los Angeles, 1953.

B. *Up in Coconino County* by Patricia Paylore. Printed by Ward Ritchie, Los Angeles, 1953.

C. *Two Kinds of People* by J. Frank Dobie. Printed by Grant Dahlstrom at the Castle Press, Pasadena, 1953.

D. *When We Peer Into the Colored Canyon* by Haniel Long. Printed by Saul and Lillian Marks at the Plantin Press, Los Angeles, 1954.

E. *Paso por Aquí* by Mary Austin. Printed by Gordon Williams on his Hand-Press in Zelzah, 1954.

F. *A Speech in the United States Senate Given on June 15, 1935,* by Henry Fountain Ashurst. Printed by Richard Hoffman, Los Angeles, 1955.

G. *What We Are Here For* by Charles F. Lummis. Printed by Lawton Kennedy, San Francisco, 1956.

H. *Bent's Fort* by David Lavender. Designed and with drawings by Merle Armitage. Printed by Cole-Holmquist, Los Angeles, 1955.

I. *Trans Pecos* by J. Frank Dobie. Printed by Carl Hertzog of El Paso, with drawings by José Cisneros, 1955.

J. *Brush Country* by J. Frank Dobie. Printed by Grant Dahlstrom at the Castle Press, Pasadena, 1956.

K. *Rivers* by Harvey Fergusson. Printed by Raphael Gonsalves and Edward A. Possnecke at Los Angeles City College under the supervision of Richard Hoffman, 1956.

L. *Land of the Southwest* by Paul Horgan. Printed by the Grabhorn Press, San Francisco, 1958.

## 1959

[21] Powell, Gertrude Clark. *The Quiet Side of Europe*. With a Memoir of the Author by Her Son Lawrence Clark Powell. Pages i–xxiii, [1]–256 plus colophon leaf, 20.5 cm x 14.7 cm. Lemon-colored cloth in acetate dust jacket.

> "250 copies printed in the Netherlands by N.V. Drukkerij of Amsterdam for presentation only." — From the colophon.
>
> In his autobiography Powell calls this work of his mother's "a happy book about her years abroad, 1931–34, the crowning time of her life." — *Fortune & Friendship*, 185.
>
> This well-integrated volume is set in rather small type, but has comfortable margins, a restrained and properly letterspaced title page, an attractive binding, and no embellishment inside or out. The mood is firmly established with a cheerful frontis portrait of Powell and his mother, radiant in her eightieth year.

## 1962

[22] Lea, Tom. *Maud Durlin Sullivan, 1872–1944: Pioneer Southwestern Librarian*. A Tribute by Tom Lea. Printed by Carl Hertzog of El Paso for the Class of 1962, School of Library Service, University of California at Los Angeles. [10] pages plus colophon leaf. 21.4 cm x 13.5 cm. Blue wrappers.

> "In 1908 Maud Durlin left the familiar green valleys of her native Wisconsin and came to West Texas, to live by the dusty edge of the Rio Bravo del Norte and become the librarian of El Paso's Public Library.
>
> "When she died thirty-five years later, by the same Rio Bravo and still El Paso's librarian, she had made with her mind and energy one of the richest contributions a good citizen ever brought to West Texas. It was a gift imponderable and impossible accurately to measure and survey, for in its most important aspect it was entirely a thing of the spirit: a force working to enlarge civilization, a gift offered to the mind. Both her life and her library were devoted to the offering of this gift. When she died, this had become not only her contribution but her reward."
>
> Thus in noble cadence begins Lea's tribute to the memory of Mrs. Sullivan. These words first appeared in the March 1944 issue of the *Library Journal*. In 1962 Hertzog reprinted them for Dean Powell in a typographical format of eloquent simplicity, consisting of Caledonia for the text and Hadriano for display.

[23] Powell, Lawrence Clark. *Go Forth And Be Useful*. Valedictory Address of the Dean to the Class of 1962, School of Library Service, University of California at Los Angeles. 8 pages plus colophon leaf. 14.3 cm x 9.8 cm. Hand-tied in light gray wrappers.

> "150 Copies Printed by W. M. Cheney, July, 1962." — From the colophon.
>
> Here is a powerful message in small format that nevertheless conveys personal

warmth without sentimentality. The use of ornaments and borders is quite effective, especially on the title page.

## 1964

[24] Powell, Lawrence Clark (ed.). *Aldous Huxley: 1894–1963*. Addresses at a Memorial Meeting Held in the School of Library Service, February 27, 1964, by Lawrence Clark Powell, Robert R. Kirsch, and Jacob Zeitlin. Los Angeles: University of California. 10 pages. 24.4 cm x 15.6 cm. Light gray wrappers.

"Printed in the Netherlands at Gouda by Koch & Knuttel N.V. as a keepsake for the Class of 1964, School of Library Service, UCLA." — From the colophon.

Here again is a straight piece of communication without trickery or cliches to distract. The title lines on the front cover are squarely centered, making them appear optically lower than they are.

[25] Powell, Lawrence Clark. *Harold Haines Clark, 1878–1964*. 9 pages plus colophon leaf. Deckled edges. 15.9 cm x 10.5 cm. Hand-tied in green wrappers.

"Eulogy spoken by Lawrence Clark Powell at memorial services held for Harold Haines Clark born January 18, 1878, at Cornwall-on-Hudson, New York, died March 27, 1964, at Santa Monica, California. Printed by Wm. M. Cheney." — From the colophon.

Eloquently rendered memorials, such as Cheney has produced here, give comfort long after flowers and music have faded.

[26] Powell, Lawrence Clark. *The Three L's*. Los Angeles: The Press in the Gatehouse. 8 pages. Deckled edges. 18.4 cm x 11.7 cm. Hand-tied in gray wrappers.

"150 copies of this address, given at the annual meeting of the Grolier Club of New York on January 23, 1964. Printed by W. M. Cheney." — From the colophon.

Despite the ebullient title page and other demonstrations of typographical expertise, the printer's ego never intrudes on the author's message.

[27] Powell, Lawrence Clark. *Viva Wagner!* Remarks by Lawrence Clark Powell at the Memorial Award Dinner given by the California Historical Society at San Francisco on September 25, 1964. Los Angeles: The Press in the Gatehouse. 10 pages plus colophon leaf. 17.5 cm x 12.3 cm. Hand-tied in tan wrappers.

"Printed by W. M. Cheney for presentation by L.C.P. to members of the Zamorano Club in recognition of H.R.W.'s 100th birthday." — From the colophon.

Like Oliver Goldsmith's Squire Hardcastle, Henry Raup Wagner loved old friends, old times, old manners, old books, old wines. His unquenchable *joie d' vivre* was best appreciated by fellow members of the Zamorano Club and E. Clampus Vitus.

Cheney's dashing treatment of Powell's light-hearted remembrance culminates in a sparkling three-color title page (of burgundy, gold, and black) which is as exhilaratingly unsubtle as the designer could get and yet remain wholly within tasteful limits.

## 1965

[28] De la Mare, Walter. *Envoi.* 14 cm x 11 cm. French-fold.

"Selected by Lawrence Clark Powell. Printed by Andrew Horn & Saul Marks for friends and admirers of Frances Clark Sayers. Rieber Hall, UCLA, 12 June 1965." — From the colophon.

There is no use of color whatever in this simple, French-fold keepsake, but the tasteful layout and immaculate presswork are exemplary.

[29] Powell, Lawrence Clark. *Words Spoken in Memory of Ralph Mac-Knight Smith (1943–1965) at a Memorial Service Held in Santa Monica, California, March 23, 1965.* 7 pages plus colophon. 19.2 cm x 12.8 cm. Hand-tied in gray wrappers.

"Printed at the Press in the Gatehouse, Los Angeles, 1965." — From the colophon.

It would be difficult to imagine a more heartrendingly beautiful format than the starkly simple one provided here by Will Cheney.

## 1966

[30] Powell, Lawrence Clark. *Come Hither!* Papers on Children's Literature and Librarianship. Los Angeles: Yeasayers Press. 40 pages plus colophon leaf. 19 cm x 13 cm. Gold-colored, double-fold wrappers.

"Printed by N.V. Drukkerij Trio, The Hague, through the good offices of Menno Hertzberger & Co., Amsterdam, The Netherlands." — From the colophon.

This collection of papers, by four of Mrs. Sayers's distinguished colleagues, was read at a farewell meeting on the occasion of her retirement from UCLA's School of Library Service. Powell edited the papers and contributed a brief foreword. The Yeasayers Press was especially created for this publication as a pun on the honoree's name.

The paper on which this tribute is printed has a texture and feel that is seldom found in American publications. The title page has much to say typographically and says it well. In every respect the format fits the personality of Mrs. Sayers — warm, gracious, and soft-spoken, but with great underlying strength.

[31] Powell, Lawrence Clark. *Musical Blood Brothers: Wolfgang Amadeus Mozart, Franz Josef Haydn.* Malibu: Press of the Prevailing Westerly. 28 pages plus colophon leaf. 19 cm x 12.8 cm. Green wrappers with printed paper label.

"These papers, given as addresses to the Zamorano Club, were printed for the author by N.V. Drukkerij Trio in The Hague, through the good offices of Menno Hertzberger & Co., of Amsterdam, as a keepsake for the joint meeting of the Roxburghe and Zamorano clubs in Los Angeles, September 1966." — From the colophon.

As Mozart and Haydn composed their own respective musical jokes in moments of levity, L.C.P. expressed his in the name of his press. The design of this keepsake is a veritable symphony of subtle taste and good craftsmanship.

## 1971

[32] Powell, Lawrence Clark. *The Three H's*. Los Angeles: The Press in the Gatehouse. Pages i–iv, [1]–9. 18.4 cm x 11.6 cm. Hand-tied in beige wrappers.

Dr. Powell's remarks were addressed initially to the Croatian Library Association at Zagreb in 1966. Five years later they were printed by Will Cheney for presentation to the graduating class at UCLA's School of Library Service.

Although both text and cover papers are a bit stiff in relation to the size and shape of the pamphlet, the usual high Cheney standards are fully evident.

## 1973

[33] Menuhin, Yehudi. *Bartok: A Memoir*. 7 pages plus colophon leaf. 20.5 cm x 13.3 cm. Hand-tied in figured paper covers.

"When I read this moving memoir in his *Theme and Variations,* I wrote to Yehudi Menuhin to ask if I might commission Saul and Lillian Marks to reprint it at their Plantin Press in Los Angeles.

"Accordingly, with his kind permission and that of his publishers, 175 copies have been made for the author, and for Fay and me to give to friends.

"I am grateful to Mary Kuper of the Plantin Press for the beautiful frontispiece wood engraving. Lawrence Clark Powell, University of Arizona, Tucson, 1973." — From the colophon.

The format of this outstanding item is itself deeply reflective and infinitely intriguing. The figured paper covers clearly evoke a rhythmic quality. The frontispiece, an elegant woodcut, depicts festive dancers. The text, set in Bembo, begins with an initial letter framed in a beautiful border. The approach is very emotional, yet restrained. It speaks of life and music, not death.

## 1974

[34] Powell, Lawrence Clark (ed.). *To Remember J. Gregg Layne, 1893–1952. A Gathering of Tributes by Fellow Bookmen*. [12] pages. 22.8 cm x 10.3 cm. Wrappers.

"It has been more than twenty years since J. Gregg Layne's death. Memory of him is still keen among those who were privileged to know and enjoy his warm friendship, gay conviviality and extensive knowledge of Western books and lore. For those members of the Zamorano and Roxburghe clubs who were not so privileged Lawrence

Clark Powell and Ward Ritchie have resurrected these expressions of regard from the *UCLA Librarian* of August 29, 1952, for those attending the 1974 Roxburghe-Zamorano gathering." — From the preface.

[35] Powell, Lawrence Clark. *W. W. Robinson, 1891–1972: Eulogy.* 7 pages plus colophon. Deckled edges. 32.4 cm x 20.7 cm. Hand-tied in binding of white paper on boards with gold stamping.

"Spoken at the memorial service for William Wilcox Robinson at the Beverly Hills Community Presbyterian Church, September 6, 1972. This eulogy is reprinted from *Hoja Volante* for the members of the Zamorano and Roxburghe clubs at their biennial reunion in Los Angeles, September 28–29, 1974.

"Composed in Caslon types, printed on all-rag hand-made paper. Paper making and printing by Zamoranans Richard Hoffman and John Urabec at California State University, Los Angeles." — From the colophon.

This small folio placed in the 1975 Western Books Exhibit of the Rounce and Coffin Club.

1975

[36] Powell, Lawrence Clark. *Vein of Silk, Vein of Steel.* Words in Memory of Saul Marks. 5 pages plus colophon leaf. 28.5 cm x 18.3 cm. Hand-tied in figured paper on boards with black cloth spine and printed title label.

"150 copies of this address by Lawrence Clark Powell given at a memorial service held at the William Andrews Clark Memorial Library on June 6, 1975, were printed by Richard J. Hoffman." — From the colophon.

Hoffman's homage to his fellow printer employs typographical elements often favored by the late Saul Marks. The title page, set in Janson, utilizes a rather delicate ornament that is reminiscent of the Marks touch, but the three-color layout is pure Hoffman. At the beginning of the text an ornate printer's device is used in lieu of a decorated initial. Adapted from that of Christopher Plantin, it is reproduced here in a brick red shade that Marks especially liked.

The text itself has been carefully composed in 14-point Bembo Monotype, which harmonizes perfectly with the Janson on the title page. This volume placed in the Western Books Exhibit for 1976.

[37] Schaefer, John P. *New Administration & Old Chemistry.* An address by John P. Schaefer, President, University of Arizona, Tucson. 11 pages plus colophon. 22.9 cm x 15.2 cm. Buff-colored wrappers.

"This address by John P. Schaefer, President and Professor of Chemistry, University of Arizona, was given at a Conference of Libraries and Scholarship sponsored by the Graduate Library School, College of Education, and the University Library, on November 22–23, 1974. Seven hundred fifty copies have been printed by the Northland Press in Flagstaff." — From the colophon.

Powell commissioned the printing of this speech as a surprise Christmas present for President Schaefer. Set in Palatino, it offers good typography devoid of frills. Unless there was a mistake in trimming, the title and author lines on the front cover would have looked better had they been centered, or somewhat left of center, rather than skewed to the right. A minor quibble, however.

# CHECKLIST OF THE PUBLISHED WRITINGS
# OF LAWRENCE CLARK POWELL
# JUNE 1966 — SEPTEMBER 1976
### Robert Mitchell

∴ℬ∴

Afterwords:

Menhuin, Yehudi. *Bartok, a Memoir.* Los Angeles: Plantin Press, 1973.
175 copies.

*Arizona, a bicentennial history.* New York: Norton, 1976.

"The Arizona Environment." *Wildcats: University of Arizona Football,* (Oct. 4, 1975),
pp.30–31.
Reprint of "An Introduction to the Arizona Environment." *Arizona Alumnus,*
(Sept. 1975).

"Arizona's Dry and Wrinkled Land." *Arizona Librarian,* Vol. 25 (Fall 1968),
pp. 12–19.
Reprinted from *Books in My Baggage.*

"A Backward Look Ahead." *The UCLA Monthly,* (Nov. 1973), pp. 5–6.

"A Backward Look by the Retiring Editor." *Books of the Southwest,* No. 109 (June,
1966), p. 1.

"Beyond the Bicentennial." *Westways,* Vol. 68, no. 3 (Mar. 1976), pp. 34–37.
Final chapter from LCP's bicentennial history of Arizona.

*Bibliographers of the Golden State.* Berkeley: University of California Press, 1967.

"Bookman's Credo" in *American Library Philosophy* selected by B. McCrimmon,
Shoestring Press, Hamden, Conn., 1975.

*Bookman's Progress: The Selected Writings of Lawrence Clark Powell.* Los Angeles:
Ward Ritchie Press, 1968.

"Books for Your Baggage." *Westways,* Vol. 58, no. 4 (April, 1968), pp. 51–54.

*Books in My Baggage: Adventures in Reading and Collecting.* Westport, Conn.:

Greenwood Press, 1973.
Reprint of 1960 edition.

*Books of the Southwest: a Critical Checklist of Current Southwestern Americana.*
Nos. 107/108–109 (April/May-June, 1966).
Lawrence Clark Powell, coeditor.

"Books of the West." *Westways,* Vol. 58, no. 1 (Jan. 1966), pp. 41–42.

"Books of the West." *Westways,* Vol. 58, no. 2 (Feb. 1966), pp. 34–35.

"Books of the West." *Westways,* Vol. 58, no. 3 (Mar. 1966), pp. 57–58.

"Books of the West." *Westways,* Vol. 58, no. 5 (May 1966), pp. 45–49.

"Books of the West." *Westways,* Vol. 58, no. 6 (June 1966), pp. 50–51.

"Books of the West." *Westways,* Vol. 58, no. 7 (July 1966), pp. 54–55.

"Books of the West." *Westways,* Vol. 58, no. 8 (Aug. 1966), pp. 50–51.

"Books of the West." *Westways,* Vol. 58, no. 9 (Sept. 1966), pp. 50–51.

"Books of the West." *Westways,* Vol. 58, no. 10 (Oct. 1966), pp. 60, 62.

"Books of the West." *Westways,* Vol. 59, no. 3 (Mar. 1967), pp. 49–51.

"Books of the West." *Westways,* Vol. 59, no. 4 (Apr. 1967), pp. 46–48.

"Books of the West." *Westways,* Vol. 59, no. 6 (June 1967), pp. 46–47.

"Books of the West." *Westways,* Vol. 59, no. 7 (July 1967), pp. 52–53.

"Books of the West." *Westways,* Vol. 59, no. 8 (Aug. 1967), pp. 50–51.

"Books of the West." *Westways,* Vol. 59, no. 9 (Sept. 1967), pp. 52–53.

"Books of the West." *Westways,* Vol. 59, no. 10 (Oct. 1967), pp. 50–51.

"Books of the West." *Westways,* Vol. 59, no. 11 (Nov. 1967), pp. 54–55.

"Books of the West." *Westways,* Vol. 59, no. 12 (Dec. 1967), pp. 48–49.

"Books of the West." *Westways,* Vol. 60, no. 1 (Jan. 1968), pp. 36–37.

"Books of the West." *Westways,* Vol. 60, no. 2 (Feb. 1968), pp. 34–35.

"Books of the West." *Westways,* Vol. 60, no. 3 (Mar. 1968), pp. 50–51.

"Books on the Gold Rush." *Westways,* Vol. 59, no. 5 (May, 1967), pp. 66–68.

*Books: West, Southwest; Essays on Writers, Their Books, and Their Land.* Westport, Conn.: Greenwood Press, 1974.
Reprint of the 1957 edition.

*California Classics: The Creative Literature of the Golden State.* Los Angeles: Ward Ritchie Press, 1971.

"California Classics Reread: *After Many a Summer Dies the Swan.*" *Westways,* Vol. 62, no. 12 (Dec. 1970), pp. 4–7, 52–53.

"California Classics Reread: *Anza's California Expeditions.*" *Westways,* Vol. 61, no. 10 (Oct. 1969), pp. 24–27, 43.

"California Classics Reread: *Boy on Horseback.*" *Westways,* Vol. 62, no. 8, (Aug. 1970), pp. 16–19, 55.

"California Classics Reread: *California and the West.*" *Westways,* Vol. 62, no. 6 (June 1970), pp. 12–15, 44.

"California Classics Reread: *California Coast Trails*." *Westways*, Vol. 61, no. 1 (Jan. 1969), pp.16–19.

"California Classics Reread: *The Cattle on a Thousand Hills*." *Westways*, Vol. 61, no. 4 (Apr. 1969), pp. 14–17, 52.

"California Classics Reread: *The Day of the Locust*." *Westways*, Vol. 62, no. 11 (Nov. 1970), pp. 12–15, 44.

"California Classics Reread: *Death Valley in '49*." *Westways*, Vol. 61, no. 11 (Nov. 1969), pp. 30–33, 52.

"California Classics Reread: *Farewell, My Lovely*." *Westways*, Vol. 61, no. 3 (Mar. 1969), pp. 6–9.

"California Classics Reread: *Give Your Heart to the Hawks*." Westways, Vol. 60, no. 11 (Nov. 1968), pp. 18–21, 58.

"California Classics Reread: *The Journey of the Flame*." *Westways*, Vol. 62, no. 7 (July 1970), pp. 16–19, 48–49.

"California Classics Reread: *The Land of Little Rain*." *Westways*, Vol. 60, no. 4 (Apr. 1968), pp. 2–4.

"California Classics Reread: *The Land of Sunshine*." *Westways*, Vol. 62, no. 1 (Jan. 1970), pp. 20–23, 35.

"California Classics Reread: *The Luck of Roaring Camp*." *Westways*, Vol. 61, no. 6 (June 1969), pp. 6–9, 48.

"California Classics Reread: *McTeague*." *Westways*, Vol. 61, no. 5 (May 1969), pp. 8–11

"California Classics Reread: *Martin Eden*." *Westways*, Vol. 61, no. 9 (Sept. 1969), pp. 10–13, 45.

"California Classics Reread: *Merton of the Movies*." *Westways*, Vol. 62, no. 10 (Oct. 1970), pp. 24–27, 66–67.

"California Classics Reread: *Mountaineering in the Sierra Nevada*." *Westways*, Vol. 62, no. 5 (May 1970), pp. 14–17, 48–49.

"California Classics Reread: *The Mountains of California*." *Westways*, Vol. 60, no. 6 (June 1968), pp. 9–11.

"California Classics Reread: *Oil!*" *Westways*, Vol. 62, no. 9 (Sept. 1970), pp. 14–17, 58–59.

"California Classics Reread: *Ramona*." *Westways*, Vol. 60, no. 7 (July 1968), pp. 13–15, 55.

"California Classics Reread: *Reminiscences of a Ranger*." *Westways*, Vol. 61, no. 2 (Feb. 1969), pp. 10–13, 41.

"California Classics Reread: *Roughing It*." *Westways*, Vol. 61, no. 7 (July 1969), pp. 19–21.

"California Classics Reread: *The Shirley Letters*." *Westways*, Vol. 61, no. 12 (Dec. 1969), pp. 26–29, 40.

"California Classics Reread: *The Silverado Squatters*." *Westways*, Vol. 60, no. 8 (Aug. 1968), pp. 22–25.

"California Classics Reread: *The Splendid Idle Forties.*" *Westways,* Vol. 60, no. 10 (Oct. 1968), pp. 22–25.

"California Classics Reread: *To a God Unknown.*" *Westways,* Vol. 60, no. 12 (Dec. 1968), pp. 18–21.

"California Classics Reread: *Two Years Before the Mast.*" *Westways,* Vol. 60, no. 5 (May 1968), pp. 12–15, 46.

"California Classics Reread: *Up and Down California.*" *Westways,* Vol 62, no. 4 (Apr. 1970), pp. 14–17, 61.

"California Classics Reread: *The Vineyard.*" *Westways,* Vol. 62, no. 3 (Mar. 1970), pp. 18–21, 52–53.

"California Classics Reread: *The Wonders of the Colorado Desert.*" *Westways,* Vol. 62, no. 2 (Feb. 1970), pp. 4–7, 52.

"Classics At Continents End." *Westways,* Vol. 63, no. 8 (Aug. 1971), pp. 8–13, 54–57.

"Climbing the Ladder." *Library Journal,* Vol. 93 (Jan. 1, 1968), pp. 49–53. A chapter from *Fortune & Friendship.*

"A Cold Look At a Hot Subject; Or Whose Library Is It?" University of Arizona, *Library Occasional Papers.* No. 1. *Service Or Organization; Two Views — Three Responses.* Papers presented at a double-session colloquim held in April, 1973, under the sponsorship of the Library and the Graduate Library School of the University of Arizona. Tucson, Ariz.: University of Arizona Library, 1973.

"A Dedication to the Memory of Mary Hunter Austin, 1868–1934." *Arizona and the West,* Vol. 10 (Spring 1968), pp. 1–4.

"The Desert." *Arizona Highways,* Vol. 50, no. 3 (Mar. 1974), pp. 2–3, 14–15. Condensed from *Southwest Classics.*

*The Desert As Dwelled On.* Los Angeles: Dawson's Book Shop, 1973.

"The Desert As Dwelled On." *Arizona Highways,* Vol. 50, no. 3 (Mar. 1974), pp.8–9. Reprint of Dawson's Book Shop edition.

"The Elements of a Good Librarian." *Occidental College Alumnus,* Vol. 49, no. 2 (Winter 1967), pp 1–7.

"The Elements of a Good Librarian." Marshall, J. D., comp., *Of, By, and For Librarians.* Second Series. Hamden, Conn.: Shoestring Press, 1974, pp. 123–33.

Epigraphs:

*AB Bookman's Weekly,* Vol. 42, no. 13 (Sept. 23, 1968), p. 1.

*AB Bookman's Weekly,* Vol. 52, no. 20 (Nov. 12, 1973), p. 1.

UCLA Graduate School of Library Service. Students Association. *Special Collections.* Los Angeles: UCLA Graduate School of Library Service Students Association, 1971.

"Epilogue." *Arizona Librarian,* Vol. 25 (Fall 1968), pp. 29–30. From *Southwestern Book Trails.*

*The Example of Miss Edith Coulter.* Keepsake No. 8. Sacramento: California Library Association, 1969.

"Exploring Arizona's Literary Trails." *Arizona Highways,* Vol. 48, no. 9 (Sept. 1972) pp. 16–23.

"The Extra Dimension." *The University Journal,* California State University, Chico, No. 5 (Spring 1976), p. 8.

"Fifty Years of Treasure: The First Half Century of Arizona Highways." *Arizona Highways,* Vol. 51, no. 4 (April 1975), pp. 60–61.

Forewords:

Bennett, Melba Berry. *The Stone Mason of Tor House; the Life and Work of Robinson Jeffers.* Los Angeles: Ward Ritchie Press, 1966.

Bieler, Henry G., and Sarah Nichols. *Dr. Bieler's Natural Way to Sexual Health.* Los Angeles: Charles Publishing Co., 1972. Paperback reprint published by Bantam Books, 1974.

Collison, Robert Lewis. *The Story of Street Literature; Forerunner of the Popular Press.* London: Dent, 1973.

Gordon, Dudley. *Charles F. Lummis: Crusader in Corduroy.* Los Angeles: Cultural Assets Press, 1972.

Hartzell, James, and Richard Zumwinkle, comps. *Kenneth Rexroth: A Checklist of His Published Writings.* Los Angeles: Friends of the UCLA Library, 1967.

Hicks, Jimmie. *W. W. Robinson; a Biography and a Bibliography.* Los Angeles: Ward Ritchie Press, 1970.

Leadabrand, Russ. *A Guidebook to the Mojave Desert of California, Including Death Valley, Joshua Tree National Monument, and the Antelope Valley.* Los Angeles: Ward Ritchie Press, 1966.

Leopold, Carolyn Clugston. *School Libraries Worth Their Keep; a Philosophy Plus Tricks.* Metuchen, N.J.: Scarecrow Press, 1972.

Magee, David Bickerstith. *Infinite Riches; the Adventures of a Rare Book Dealer.* New York: Paul S. Eriksson, 1973.

Mori, Haruhide, ed. *A Conversation On D. H. Lawrence.* Los Angeles: Friends of the UCLA Library, 1974.

Thompson, Lawrence Sidney. *Books In Our Time; Essays by Lawrence S. Thompson.* Washington: Consortium Press, 1972.

Turner, Chittenden. *Poems and Light Verse.* Sherman Oaks, Cal.: Pen-n-Quill, 1973.

Weber, Francis J. *A Select Bibliography to California Catholic Literature 1856–1974.* Los Angeles: Dawson's Book Shop, 1974.

*Fortune & Friendship: An Autobiography.* New York: R. R. Bowker Co., 1968.

"Graduate School of Library Science, The University of Arizona." *Fifth Annual Report.* Tucson, Ariz.: The President's Club of the University of Arizona, 1972.

"Great Land of Libraries." Marshall, J. D,. comp. *Of, By, and For Librarians.* Second Series. Hamden, Conn.: Shoestring Press, 1974.
Reprint from *ALA Bulletin* (July 1965), pp. 643–48.

"Henry Miller At Eighty." *Westways,* Vol. 64, no. 4 (Apr. 1972), pp. 26–29, 58–60.

"An Introduction to the Arizona Environment." *Arizona Alumnus,* Vol. 53, no. 1 (Sept. 1975), pp. 27–30.

"Jeffers." Dutton, Davis, and Judy Dutton, eds. *Tales of Monterey*. New York: Ballantine, 1974. pp. 137–147.
From *California Classics*.

"John E. Goodwin: Founder of the UCLA Library; an Essay Toward a Biography." *Journal of Library History*, Vol. 6 (July 1971), pp. 265–74.

"John E. Goodwin: Founder of the UCLA Library; an Essay Toward a Biography." *Vignettes of Library History*, No. 10. Los Angeles: Friends of UCLA Library, 1972. Reprint of the *Journal of Library History* article.

"Land of Many Returns." *New Mexico Magazine*, Vol. 52, no. 5-6 (May–June 1974), pp. 11–15.

"Landscape With Books." *Arizona Librarian*, Vol. 25 (Fall 1968), pp. 6–11.
From *The Southwest of the Bookman*.

"Letter From the Southwest." *Westways*, Vol. 66, no. 11 (Nov. 1974), pp. 32–34.

"Letter from the Southwest." *Westways*, Vol. 67, no. 1 (Jan. 1975), pp. 22–26.

"Letter from the Southwest." *Westways*, Vol. 67, no. 3 (Mar. 1975), pp. 18–21.

"Letter from the Southwest." *Westways*, Vol. 67, no. 5 (May 1975), pp. 38–41.

"Letter from the Southwest." *Westways*, Vol. 67, no. 7 (July 1975), pp. 24–27.

"Letter from the Southwest." *Westways*, Vol. 67, no. 9 (Sept. 1975), pp. 32–34, 79.

Letters to the Editor:
*American Libraries*, Vol. 2, no. 7 (July–Aug. 1971), p. 682.
*American Libraries*, Vol. 3, no. 9 (Oct. 1972), pp. 960–61.

*The Little Package; Pages on Literature and Landscape from a Travelling Bookman's Life*. Freeport, N.Y.: Books for Libraries Press, 1971.
Reprint of 1964 ed.

*Looking Back at Sixty: Recollections of L.C.P., Librarian, Writer, Teacher*. Interviewed by James V. Mink. Oral History Program, University of California, Los Angeles. Los Angeles, 1973. Restricted during L.C.P.'s lifetime.

"Los Angeles Bibliography." Johnson Paul C., ed. *Los Angeles: Portrait of an Extraordinary City*. Menlo Park, Cal.: Lane Magazine & Book Co., 1968, pp. 300–302.

"Los Angeles Bibliography." Reprint, "expanded to include additional trade information for this printing," by the Southern California Booksellers Association. n.d.

*The Manuscripts of D. H. Lawrence; a Descriptive Catalogue*. New York: Gordon Press, 1972.
Reprint of 1937 ed.

"Margaret Girdner." *California Librarian*, Vol. 31, no. 3 (July 1970), pp. 210–11.

"Melba Berry Bennett." *Robinson Jeffers Newsletter*, No. 23 (April 1969) p. 1.

"Melba Berry Bennett" *Melba Berry Bennett*. Printed for Theodore M. Lilienthal at the Ward Ritchie Press [1969] pp. [8–9.]

"Memo to Jake Zeitlin." Edelstein, J. M., ed. *A Garland for Jake Zeitlin on the Occa-*

*sion of His 65th Birthday & the Anniversary of His 40th Year in the Book Trade.*
Los Angeles: Grant Dahlstrom & Saul Marks, 1967, pp.33–38.

"Musical Blood Brothers." Boaz, Martha, comp. *The Quest for Truth*, Vol. 2, *The Continuing Quest.* Metuchen, N.J.: Scarecrow Press, 1967, pp. 70–81.

"The Mystique Endures." *Westways*, Vol. 65, no. 6 (June 1973), pp. 26–31, 92–93.

"Northland Press in the Pinewood." *Arizona Librarian*, Vol. 25 (Fall 1968), pp. 20–28. From *The Little Package.*

"Oak-wooded Malibu." Robinson, W. W. comp. *Zamorano Choice; Selections from the Zamorano Club's Hoja Volante 1943–1966.* Los Angeles: The Zamorano Club, 1966, pp. 58–61.
Reprint of two articles: "Oak Grove Summer," *Hoja Volante* (Nov. 1959); and "Oak Grove Winter," *Hoja Volante* (Feb. 1960).

"Olé Olin." *Wesleyan Library Notes*, No. 1 (Autumn 1968), pp. 2–4.

*A Passion for Books.* Westport, Conn.: Greenwood Press, 1973.
Reprint of 1958 ed.

"Personalities of the West: The Adventurous Englishman." *Westways*, Vol. 65, no. 11 (Nov. 1973), pp. 18–22, 70–71.

"Personalities of the West: Maynard Dixon's Painted Desert." *Westways*, Vol. 66, no. 5 (May, 1974), pp. 24–29, 86–87.

"Personalities of the West: Mr. Bookseller." *Westways*, Vol. 66, no. 7 (July 1974), pp. 26–31, 67.

"Personalities of the West: A Nice Place to Visit." *Westways*, Vol. 65, no. 9 (Sept. 1973), pp. 36–39, 66, 68–69.

"Personalities of the West: A Singular Ranger." *Westways*, Vol. 66, no. 3 (Mar. 1974), pp. 32–35, 64–65.

"Personalities of the West: A Writer's Landscape." *Westways*, Vol. 66, no. 1 (Jan. 1974), pp. 24–27, 70–72.

"Personalities of the West: A Yorkshireman Wanders West." *Westways*, Vol. 66, no. 9 (Sept. 1974), pp. 18–21, 76–77.

*Photographs of the Southwest.* Photographs by Ansel Adams and an essay on the land by Lawrence Clark Powell. New York: New York Graphic Society, 1976.

*Poems of Walt Whitman: Leaves of Grass.* Powell, Lawrence Clark, ed. New York: Thomas Y. Crowell Co., 1971.
Paperback reprint of 1964 ed.

"Printing Was His Art." *Westways*, Vol. 67, no. 11 (Nov. 1975), pp. 22–24, 84.

"Ralph D. Cornell and UCLA." *California Horticultural Journal*, Vol. 33, no. 4 (Oct. 1972), p. 135.

"Reading San Diego." Dutton, Davis, ed. *San Diego and the Back Country.* New York: Ballantine Books, 1972, pp. 187–206.
Reprints selections on San Diego from *Westways* articles circa 1948–1967.

*Remarks on the Occasion of the Dedication of Addition to the Mary Norton Clapp Library*. Los Angeles: Occidental College, 1971.

"Remembering Bob Sproul." *California Monthly*, Vol. 86, no. 2 (Nov. 1975), p. 7.

Reviews:

Brophy, Robert J., *Robinson Jeffers: Myth, Ritual and Symbol in His Narrative Poems. Southwest Review*. Vol. 59, no. 2 (Spring 1974), pp. 196–97.

Clark, Harry, *A Venture in History: The Production, Publication, and Sales of the Works of Hubert Howe Bancroft. The Library Quarterly*, Vol. 44, no. 4 (Oct. 1974) p. 361.

Colley, Charles, comp. *Documents of Southwestern History: A Guide to the Manuscripts Collections of the Arizona Historical Society. The Papers of the Bibliographical Society of America*, Vol. 67 (4th Quarter, 1967), pp. 472–74.

Downs, Robert B., *Books That Changed America. The Library Quarterly*, Vol. 40, no. 4 (Oct. 1970), pp. 448–49.

Jackson, W. A., *Records of a Bibliographer; Selected Papers. Journal of Library History*, Vol. 3 (Jan. 1968), pp. 75–77.

Jeffers, Robinson. *Cawdor and Medea. California Librarian*, Vol. 32, no. 1 (Jan. 1971), pp. 75–76.

Lowman, Al, comp., *Printer at the Pass: The Work of Carl Hertzog. Southwestern Historical Quarterly* (Oct. 1973), p. 279.

Maxwell, Margaret. *Shaping a Library: William L. Clements as Collector. The Papers of the Bibliographic Society of America*, Vol. 69 (1975), pp. 589–90.

Randall, David A., *Dukedom Large Enough. Library Journal*, Vol. 94 (Sept. 15, 1969), pp. 3030–31.

Rhodehamel, Josephine DeWitt, and Raymond Francis Wood. *Ina Coolbrith, Librarian and Laureate of California. California Librarian*, Vol. 35, no. 1 (Jan. 1974), p. 60

Targ, William, comp., *Carrousel for Bibliophiles. Library Journal*, Vol. 93 (Oct. 1, 1968), p. 3522.

"Speaking of Books: The Grand Obsession." *New York Times Book Review* (Mar. 10, 1968), pp. 2, 24.

"Speaking of Books: The Horgan File." *New York Times Book Review* (May 14, 1967), pp. 2, 40.

"Speaking of Books: Robinson Jeffers." *New York Times Book Review* (Oct. 6, 1968), pp. 2, 26.

"Things We Need to Know." *New York Times Book Review* (Nov. 5, 1967), pp. 2–3, 68–69.

"'Revista Nueva Mexicana." Hartley, Margaret L., ed. *The Southwest Review Reader*. Dallas: Southern Methodist University Press, 1974.

Reprint of an article originally published in *Southwest Review* (Winter 1957).

"Revista Nueva Mexicana." *Southwest Review*, Vol. 59, no. 4 (Autumn 1974), pp. 559–67.

Originally published in *Southwest Review* (Winter 1957).

Robinson Jeffers: The Man and His Work. Los Angeles: Primavera Press; New York: Haskell House, 1970.
  Reprint of 1934 ed.

"Shoe on the Other Foot: From Library Administrator to User." *Wilson Library Bulletin,* Vol. 45 (Dec. 1970), pp. 384–89.

*The Silverado Squatters — Robert Louis Stevenson.* St. Helena, Cal.: Norman and Charlotte Strouse, 1971.
  Reprinted from *California Classics.*

*Some thoughts on the Republication of Frederick Hastings Ridnge's Happy Days in Southern California (1898).* Los Angeles: Malibu Historical Society, 1972.

*Song of the Southwest.* Los Angeles: Southern California Historical Society, 1973.
  Reprint of article "Southwest Classics Reread: Songs of the Southwest." *Westways* (May 1973).

"South From Lisbon." *Southwest Review,* Vol. 53, no. 2 (Spring 1968), pp. 179–85.

*South From Lisbon.* Dallas: Southern Methodist University Press, 1968.
  Reprinted from *Southwest Review* (Spring 1968).

*Southwest Classics: The Creative Literature of the Arid Lands.* Los Angeles: Ward Ritchie Press, 1974.

*Southwest Classics: The Creative Literature of the Arid Lands.* Pasadena: Ward Ritchie Press, 1974.
  2d corrected printing.

"Southwest Classics Reread: *Adventures in the Apache Country.*" *Westways,* Vol. 63. no. 10 (Oct. 1971), pp. 18–21, 40–43.

"Southwest Classics Reread: *Commerce of the Prairies.*" *Westways,* Vol. 63, no. 5 (May 1971), pp. 14–17, 68–70.

"Southwest Classics Reread: *Coronado's Children.*" *Westways,* Vol. 63, no. 2 (Feb. 1971), pp. 10–13, 56–57.

"Southwest Classics Reread: *Dancing Gods.*" *Westways,* Vol. 63, no. 3 (Mar. 1971), pp. 13–17, 62.

"Southwest Classics Reread: *Death Comes for the Archbishop.*" *Westways,* Vol. 64, no. 2 (Feb. 1972), pp. 22–25, 33, 60–61.

"Southwest Classics Reread: *The Desert.*" *Westways,* Vol. 64, no. 3 (Mar. 1972), pp. 29–31, 70–71.

"Southwest Classics Reread: *The Desert Year.*" *Westways,* Vol. 63, no. 6 (June, 1971), pp. 14–17, 66–67.

"Southwest Classics Reread: The Fathers of Pimeria Alta." *Westways,* Vol. 64, no. 11 (Nov. 1972), pp. 26–30, 69.

"Southwest Classics Reread: From Cattle Kingdom Come." *Westways,* Vol. 65, no. 4 (Apr. 1973), pp. 30–35, 85.

"Southwest Classics Reread: How He Pictured the West." *Westways,* Vol. 65, no. 3 (Mar. 1973), pp. 46–50, 84.

"Southwest Classics Reread: *Interlinear to Cabeza de Vaca.*" *Westways,* Vol. 63, no. 4 (Apr. 1971), pp. 26–29, 78–79.

"Southwest Classics Reread: Lady of Taos." *Westways,* Vol. 65, no. 1 (Jan. 1973), pp. 50–53, 64–65.

"Southwest Classics Reread: A Land to Know, a West to Love." *Westways,* Vol. 64, no. 12 (Dec. 1972), pp. 28–31, 50, 52–53.

"Southwest Classics Reread: *Laughing Boy.*" *Westways,* Vol. 63, no. 12 (Dec. 1971), pp. 22–24, 50–52.

"Southwest Classics Reread: The Man Who Ran the River." *Westways,* Vol. 64, no. 6 (June 1972), pp. 36–39, 50–51.

"Southwest Classics Reread: Massacre and Vengeance in Apacheria." *Westways,* Vol. 64, no. 5 (May 1972), pp. 55–59.

"Southwest Classics Reread: *The Plumed Serpent.*" *Westways,* Vol. 63, no. 11 (Nov. 1971), pp. 18–20, 46–49.

"Southwest Classics Reread: A Prophetic Passage." *Westways,* Vol. 65, no. 2 (Feb. 1973), pp. 60–65.

"Southwest Classics Reread: *Sky Determines.*" *Westways,* Vol. 63, no. 9 (Sept. 1971), pp. 18–21, 64.

"Southwest Classics Reread: Song of the Southwest." *Westways,* Vol. 65, no. 5 (May 1973), pp. 44–47, 82–87.

"Southwest Classics Reread: Two for the Santa Fe Trail." *Westways,* Vol. 64, no. 10 (Oct. 1972), pp. 56–59, 73–74.

"Southwest Classics Reread: *Vanished Arizona.*" *Westways,* Vol. 63, no. 7 (July 1971), pp. 16–19, 60–61.

"Southwest Classics Reread: When Teddy Went West." *Westways,* Vol. 64, no. 7 (July 1972), pp. 51, 56–57, 73–74.

"Southwest Classics Reread: Wolf Song." Westways, Vol. 64, no. 1 (Jan. 1972), pp. 22–24, 41.

"Southwest Classics Reread: Writer of the Purple Page." *Westways,* Vol. 64, no. 8 (Aug. 1972), pp. 50–55, 69.

"The Southwest of the Travelling Reader." *Hoja Volante,* No. 117 (Aug. 1974), pp. 3–8.

"The Southwest of the Travelling Reader." *Occidental,* Vol. 4, no. 5 (Summer 1974), pp. 13–15.

"Talk at Antiquarian Booksellers Banquet, Ambassador Hotel, Los Angeles, October 14, 1970." *AB Bookman's Weekly,* Vol. 46 (Nov. 2, 1970), pp. 1283–1286.

[Theodore M. Lilienthal] in Roxburghe & Zamorano Clubs, 1972, p. [11].

*The Three H's.* Los Angeles: Press in the Gatehouse, 1971.

"The Three L's." In Collectors' Institute Commemorative Brochure, Austin, Texas, Nov. 23, 1968, pp. 2–6.

*To D.C. Subject: The L.C. From L.C.P.* Los Angeles. The Gatehouse Press, 1968.

*To Newbury to Buy an Old Book*. Edinburgh, The Tragara Press, 1973. Reprinted from *Books In My Baggage*.

*To Remember J. Gregg Layne, 1893–1952*. Los Angeles: Ward Ritchie Press: 1974. Reprinted from *UCLA Librarian* (August 29, 1952).

"To Visit Monterey." *Westways*, Vol. 68, no. 1 (Jan. 1976), pp. 23–26.

"A Tribute to a Mere Magazine by a Great Man." *Arizona Highways*, Vol. 47, no. 12 (Dec. 1971), p. 48.
Reprinted from *Books West Southwest*.

"A Tribute to Bradford Booth." *Modern Fiction Studies*, Vol. 16, no. 2 (Summer 1970), pp. 111–15.

*A Tribute to Bradford Booth*. Los Angeles: Friends of the UCLA Library, 1971. Reprint of the article in *Modern Fiction Studies* (Summer 1970).

*The Untarnished Gold, the Immutable Treasure; a Report of a Book-in-Progress*. Library Associates of the University Library, Davis, *Keepsake* No. 3. Davis, Cal.: University of California, Davis, 1970.

"A Valentine to Gertrude Stein." *Westways*, Vol. 66, no. 2 (Feb. 1974), pp. 18–22, 68.

*Vein of Silk, Vein of Steel; Words in Memory of Saul Marks*. Los Angeles: n.p., 1975.

"West View: Dean of Western Letters Pushed His Own Cart." *Los Angeles Times Book Review* (Apr. 20, 1975), p. 3.

"Who Is B. Traven?" North, Joseph, ed. *New Masses; an Anthology of the Rebel Thirties*. New York: International Publishers, 1969, pp. 301–6.
Reprint from *New Masses* (Aug. 2, 1938).

"W. W. Robinson, 1891–1972." *Westways*, Vol. 64, no. 10 (Oct. 1972), pp. 2, 4. Abridged version of the eulogy that appeared in full in *Hoja Volante* (Nov. 1972).

"W. W. Robinson (1891–1972)." *Hoja Volante*, No. 110 (Nov. 1972) pp. 1–2.

*W. W. Robinson, 1891–1972*. Los Angeles: Dawsons, 1974. Reprint of the *Hoja Volante* (Nov. 1972) article.

### Material About Lawrence Clark Powell

"Special Convocation on June 11 at UCLA Honored Lawrence Clark Powell." *Antiquarian Bookman*, Vol. 38 (July 4–11, 1966), p. 58.

"Bibliography of Lawrence Clark Powell's Books In Print." *Arizona Libraries*, Vol. 25, no. 3 (Fall 1968), p. 30.

Castagna, E. "Larry Powell, What Now?" *California Librarian*, Vol. 27 (July 1966), pp. 187–88.

———. *Three Who Met the Challenge: Joseph L. Wheeler, Lawrence Clark Powell, Frances Clarke Sayers*. Berkeley: Peacock Press, 1965.

Dick, Hugh G. "Lawrence Clark Powell, Librarian" in *UCLA Librarian*, Vol. 19, no. 6 (June 1966), pp. [53]–54.

Dillon, Richard H. "California's Maverick Librarians." *Quarterly Newsletter of the Book Club of California*, Vol. 38, nos. 1 & 2 (Winter 1972, Spring 1973), pp. 3–16, 35–42.

Grebanier, Bernard. Letter, *New York Times Book Review*, Nov. 10, 1968, p. 52.

Horgan, Paul. Letter, *New York Times Book Review,* June 25, 1967, pp. 32–33.

Kister, K. F. "Interview With Lawrence Clark Powell." *Bay State Librarian,* Vol. 57 (Oct. 1968), pp. 5–11. (?)

Larkey, Joann. "Davis Revisited: Lawrence Clark Powell," in *Putah Creek Letter,* Vol. 1, no. 2, (Apr. 1970), pp. 1–2.

"Lawrence Clark Powell" in *The UCLA Alumni Association Occasional Paper #4,* (Spring–Summer 1972), p. [4].

"LCP" University of Arizona. Graduate Library School. Library Students Organization. Tucson, 1973.
A T-shirt bearing the likeness of LCP which appears on the Fall 1968 cover of *Arizona Libraries.*

"Lawrence Clark Powell Has Been Awarded the Honarary Degree of Doctor of Humanities by the University of Arizona, Tucson." *Library Journal,* Vol. 96 (Oct. 15, 1971), p. 3275.

"Lawrence Clark Powell Named a Fellow to the Center for Advanced Studies at Wesleyan University, Middletown, Connecticut." *Library Journal,* Vol 93 (Feb. 15, 1967), p. 700.

"Lawrence Clark Powell Will Receive the Annual Distinguished Achievement Award Presented by the Graduate School of Library Science at the Library School Alumni Association at Drexel. *Library Journal,* Vol. 93 (Feb. 15, 1967), p. 709.

"Library Named at UCLA for Lawrence Clark Powell." *Library Journal,* Vol. 92 (Jan. 1, 1967), p. 46.

Maxwell, Margaret. "What Makes a Rare Book." *Wilson Library Bulletin,* Vol. 48 (Nov. 1973), pp. 255–56.

Mitchell, Robert. "Meet the Faculty: Lawrence Clark Powell." *Footnotes,* (a publication of the Library Students Organization, University of Arizona) Vol. 4, no. 1 (Oct. 1974), pp. 2–3.

Paylore, Patricia. "A Time to Every Purpose." *Arizona Libraries,* Vol. 25, no. 3 (Fall 1968), pp. 3–5.

"Distinguished Achievement Award Will Be Presented to Lawrence Clark Powell." *Publisher's Weekly,* Vol. 192 (Dec. 25, 1967), p. 34.

Rosenberg, Betty, comp. *Checklist of the Published Writings of Lawrence Clark Powell.* Los Angeles: Library, UCLA, 1966.

Schuman, Marilyn. "Dr. Lawrence Clark Powell puts shoe on other foot" in *The Colorado Academic Library,* Vol. 6, no. 2 (Spring 1970), pp. 12–14.

Simmons, Marc. "Book Trails and Burro Shoes: A Tribute to Lawrence Clark Powell." *Book Talk,* Vol. 3, no. 1 (Apr. 1974), p. 4.

Stacey, Joseph. "No Mere Man!" *Arizona Highways,* Vol. 48, no. 9 (Sept. 1972), p. 39.

Stevens, Norman D. " A Computer Analysis of Library Postcards (CALP)." *Journal of the American Society for Information Science,* (Sept.–Oct. 1974), pp. 332–35.

"The Story of the UCLA Library." The UCLA Alumni Association *Occasional Paper* No. 4 (Spring–Summer 1972), pp. 1–8.

"Honors Convocation Speaker." University of Arizona College of Education. *Student and Faculty Periscope* (Nov. 1974), p. 1.

"Powell to Write Arizona History for '76 Series." University of Arizona. *Faculty and Staff Newsletter,* Vol. 8, no. 2 (Oct. 1974), p. 7.

Vosper, Robert. "LCP and the Clark." Miner, Earl, ed. *Stuart and Georgian Moments; Festschrift in Honor of Lawrence Clark Powell.* Publications of the 17th and 18th Centuries Studies Group, UCLA 3. Berkeley: University of California Press, 1972, pp. xxi–xxiv.

"Lawrence Clark Powell Will Receive the Distinguished Achievement Award." *Wilson Library Bulletin,* Vol. 42 (Feb. 1968), p. 562.

### Reviews of Lawrence Clark Powell's Books

*Bookman's Progress:*

   *Booklist and Subscription Books Bulletin,* Vol. 64 (June 15, 1968), pp. 1554–56.

   Kohn, M. R., *California Librarian,* Vol. 29 (July 1968), p. 221.

   Marshall, J. D., *Journal of Library History,* Vol. 4, (July 1969), pp. 284–86.

   Nielsen, T., *Scandanavian Public Library Quarterly,* Vol. 3, no. 2 (1970), p. 106.

   Piternick, George, "Powelliana." *Library Journal,* Vol. 93, no. 16 (Sept. 15, 1968), p. 3106.

*Bookman's Progress and Fortune & Friendship:*

   Hartley, Margaret L., "Progress of a Passionate Bookman." *Southwest Review,* Vol. 53, no. 4 (Autumn 1968), pp. v–vi, 440.

*California Classics:*

   Hartley, Margaret L., "Golden State Books and Their Authors." *Southwest Review,* Vol. 58, no. 2 (Spring 1973), pp. 190–92.

*Fortune & Friendship:*

   *AB Bookman's Weekly,* Vol. 42 (Sept. 23, 1968), pp. 975–76.

   Aitken, W. R., "Once Handled, Never Forgotten." *Library Review,* Vol. 21, no. 8 (Winter 1968), pp. 417–18.

   *Indian Librarian,* Vol. 23 (Sept. 1968), pp. 132–34.

   Kohn, M. R., *California Librarian,* Vol. 30 (Jan. 1969), p. 62.

   Lund, B., *Scandanavian Public Library Quarterly,* Vol. 3, nos. 3–4 (1970), pp. 189–90.

   Marshall, J. D., *Journal of Library History,* Vol. 4 (Jan. 1969), pp. 74–76.

   Robinson, W. W., Bibliographic Society of America, *Papers,* Vol. 63 (Oct. 1969), pp. 346–47.

   Sayers, Frances Clarke, "Passionate Bookman." *Library Journal,* Vol. 93, no. 13 (July 1968), pp. 2624–25.

   Stokes, Roy, *Library Association Record,* Vol. 70, no. 11 (Nov. 1968), p. 296.

   Weintraub, B., *Drexel Library Quarterly,* Vol. 5 (Apr. 1969), pp. 126–27.

   Winger, Howard, *Library Quarterly,* Vol. 39, no. 1 (Jan. 1969), p. 120.

*Southwest Classics:*

Kirsch, Robert, "Southwest: Cradle to Creativity." Los Angeles *Times,* Jan. 13, 1975, pt. IV, p. 7.

Tinkle, Lon, "Landmark Books From Our Region." Dallas *Morning News* (Nov. 10, 1974), p. 9 F. *(Southwest Classics)*

Wilson, Maggie, "Authors Ties to Arizona Remembered." Arizona *Republic,* Jan. 11, 1975.

VOICES FROM THE SOUTHWEST
WAS DESIGNED BY JOHN ANDERSON,
EDITED BY JIM HOWARD, SET IN
12-POINT GRANJON, PRINTED ON
CLASSIC LAID TEXT AT PAUL WEAVER'S
NORTHLAND PRESS, AND BOUND BY
MARK AND IRIS ROSWELL IN PHOENIX.